The History of Canada

From Maple Leafs to Mountaintops

Copyright © 2023 by Vanessa Davis-Wilson and Einar Felix Hansen.

All rights reserved. No part of this publication may be reproduced, stored in a retrieval system, or transmitted, in any form or by any means, electronic, mechanical, photocopying, recording, or otherwise, without the prior written permission of the copyright holder. This book was created with the help of Artificial Intelligence technology.

The contents of this book are intended for entertainment purposes only. While every effort has been made to ensure the accuracy and reliability of the information presented, the author and publisher make no warranties or representations as to the accuracy, completeness, or suitability of the information contained herein. The information presented in this book is not intended as a substitute for professional advice, and readers should consult with qualified professionals in the relevant fields for specific advice.

Land of the Indigenous Peoples 6

The Dawn of Exploration 9

Jacques Cartier and the French Settlements 12

The British Dominion and the Seven Years' War 15

The American Revolution's Impact on Canada 18

The War of 1812 and Its Consequences 21

The Fur Trade and the Hudson's Bay Company 24

Confederation and the Birth of Canada 27

The Canadian Pacific Railway and Westward Expansion 30

The Klondike Gold Rush 33

The Boer War and Canadian Identity 36

Canada in World War I 39

The Roaring Twenties and the Great Depression 42

World War II and Canada's Role 45

Post-War Canada: The Baby Boom and Economic Growth 48

The Quiet Revolution in Quebec 51

The Canadian Charter of Rights and Freedoms 54

Aboriginal Rights and Land Claims 57

The National Energy Program and the Oil Crisis 61

Canada-US Relations: NAFTA and Beyond 64

Multiculturalism and Immigration 67

Women's Rights and Feminism in Canada 70

Quebec Separatism and the Referendums 73

Canada's Healthcare System: Achievements and Challenges 76

Environmentalism and Conservation Efforts 79

The Arctic: Challenges and Opportunities 82

Canada's National Parks and Natural Wonders 85

Canadian Cuisine: From Poutine to Nanaimo Bars 88

Exploring Canada: From the Rockies to the Maritimes 91

Niagara Falls and Other Iconic Landmarks 94

Vancouver: A Vibrant City on the West Coast 97

Ottawa: The Capital City and Its Historic Sites 100

Conclusion 103

Land of the Indigenous Peoples

Canada, known today as a vast and diverse nation, has a rich and complex history that predates the arrival of European settlers. It is a land that was first inhabited by Indigenous peoples, who have deep ancestral ties to the land that stretch back thousands of years. This chapter delves into the vibrant and diverse cultures of the Indigenous peoples who called Canada home long before colonization.

The Indigenous peoples of Canada are composed of numerous distinct nations, each with their own unique traditions, languages, and belief systems. They had developed thriving societies and sophisticated systems of governance, well-adapted to their environments. From the Inuit of the Arctic to the Haida of the Pacific Northwest, and the Mi'kmaq of the Atlantic region to the Cree of the Great Plains, the Indigenous peoples exhibited remarkable diversity in their ways of life.

These Indigenous communities had deep connections to the land and lived in harmony with nature. They possessed extensive knowledge of their territories, which allowed them to survive and thrive in diverse ecological settings. Through hunting, gathering, fishing, and agriculture, they sustained themselves and fostered complex social structures rooted in kinship ties and communal values.

Before the arrival of Europeans, trade networks were established among Indigenous peoples, facilitating the exchange of goods, ideas, and cultural practices across vast distances. These networks played a crucial role in shaping the social, economic, and cultural dynamics of Indigenous societies.

The Indigenous peoples also had diverse spiritual and belief systems, often intertwined with their understanding of the natural world. Their traditions and ceremonies reflected a deep reverence for the land and its resources. The vision quests, sweat lodges, and potlatches were integral to their spiritual and social fabric, fostering community cohesion and individual growth.

However, the arrival of European explorers and settlers marked a significant turning point in the history of Canada's Indigenous peoples. While the initial interactions between the Indigenous peoples and Europeans were often characterized by curiosity and trade, these encounters ultimately led to profound changes in the Indigenous way of life.

European contact brought diseases such as smallpox, measles, and influenza, to which the Indigenous peoples had no immunity. Devastating epidemics swept through their communities, resulting in significant population decline and the loss of invaluable cultural knowledge.

Furthermore, as European colonization intensified, the Indigenous peoples faced encroachment on their lands and the imposition of foreign systems of governance. The treaties signed between Indigenous nations and the European colonial powers varied in their terms and interpretations, leading to significant challenges and conflicts over land rights and self-determination.

The forced assimilation policies, such as residential schools, implemented by the Canadian government in the

19th and 20th centuries had a devastating impact on Indigenous communities. These policies aimed to erase Indigenous cultures, languages, and identities, leading to intergenerational trauma that persists to this day.

In recent years, there has been a growing recognition of the injustices and hardships experienced by Indigenous peoples. Efforts towards reconciliation and the revitalization of Indigenous languages and cultures have gained momentum. Land claims and self-governance agreements have been negotiated, empowering Indigenous communities to reclaim their heritage and assert their rights.

Canada's journey towards reconciliation is ongoing, and it is essential to acknowledge and respect the rich heritage and contributions of the Indigenous peoples. Their enduring presence and resilience continue to shape the cultural fabric of the country, enriching its diversity and providing a foundation for understanding and appreciation of Canada's complex history.

As we explore the chapters to come, we will delve deeper into the events, people, and transformative moments that have shaped the history of Canada, ultimately leading to the diverse and inclusive society it is today.

The Dawn of Exploration

The dawn of exploration in Canada marks a period of discovery, adventure, and curiosity as European nations sought to expand their knowledge and influence across the globe. This chapter delves into the explorations that took place in the early years of contact between Europeans and the lands that would later become Canada.

One of the earliest European explorers to set foot on Canadian soil was the Norse Viking Leif Erikson. Around the year 1000, Erikson, son of Erik the Red, is believed to have reached a place he called Vinland, which is thought to be present-day Newfoundland. While the Norse settlements in Vinland did not endure, Erikson's voyage represents one of the earliest known European encounters with North America.

Several centuries later, in the late 15th century, the Age of Exploration was in full swing. European powers, most notably Spain, Portugal, France, and England, embarked on ambitious voyages to seek new trade routes, riches, and territories. These expeditions were driven by a desire to establish dominance in the lucrative spice trade and expand the influence of their respective empires.

The first documented European explorer to reach Canada's eastern shores was John Cabot, an Italian navigator sailing under the English flag. In 1497, Cabot arrived in what is now Newfoundland, likely in the vicinity of Cape Bonavista. His voyage opened the door to further English exploration and laid the foundation for future English claims to North America.

Following Cabot's expedition, French explorers began making their way to the North American continent. Jacques Cartier, a French navigator, embarked on three voyages between 1534 and 1542, venturing into the Gulf of St. Lawrence and exploring areas that would become part of modern-day Canada. Cartier's voyages were instrumental in establishing French claims and laying the groundwork for future French settlements.

Explorers from other European nations also played a role in the early exploration of Canada. In 1576, Martin Frobisher, an English explorer, made several voyages to the Arctic region in search of the Northwest Passage, a fabled trade route to Asia. Although Frobisher's attempts to find the passage were unsuccessful, his expeditions contributed to European knowledge of the northern reaches of Canada.

Throughout the 17th century, French explorers and fur traders, known as coureurs des bois, ventured deep into the interior of North America. Samuel de Champlain, often referred to as the "Father of New France," explored and mapped large portions of the St. Lawrence River and the Great Lakes region. Champlain's efforts laid the foundation for French colonization and the establishment of Quebec, the first permanent French settlement in Canada.

As European exploration continued, significant encounters and interactions took place between the explorers and the Indigenous peoples of the land. These interactions varied from friendly alliances and trade partnerships to clashes and conflicts over resources and territories. Indigenous peoples played an integral role in assisting explorers with their knowledge of the land, acting as guides and facilitators of trade.

The dawn of exploration in Canada set the stage for subsequent waves of colonization and the eventual shaping of Canada's cultural and political landscape. The explorations of the 15th to 17th centuries not only expanded European knowledge of North America but also laid the groundwork for the establishment of colonies and the eventual conflicts that would arise among European powers.

The legacy of these early explorations is complex and multifaceted. While they contributed to the expansion of European influence and the formation of modern-day Canada, they also had far-reaching consequences for Indigenous peoples, leading to profound changes in their societies and ways of life.

Jacques Cartier and the French Settlements

Jacques Cartier, a French explorer, played a significant role in the early exploration and colonization of Canada. His voyages, spanning from 1534 to 1542, laid the foundation for French claims in North America and opened the door to future French settlements. This chapter delves into Cartier's expeditions and the establishment of French presence in Canada.

In 1534, King Francis I of France commissioned Jacques Cartier to find a westward passage to Asia and expand French influence in the New World. Cartier embarked on his first voyage, which led him to the eastern coast of North America. He explored the Gulf of St. Lawrence and made contact with the Indigenous peoples inhabiting the region. Cartier claimed the land for France and named it "Canada," derived from the Iroquoian word "kanata," meaning village or settlement.

Encouraged by his initial discoveries, Cartier embarked on a second voyage in 1535. He sailed up the St. Lawrence River, becoming the first European to navigate this vital waterway. Along his journey, Cartier encountered several Indigenous communities, including the Iroquoian-speaking St. Lawrence Iroquoians and the Innu. He established friendly relations with some groups while encountering resistance and hostilities from others.

Cartier reached the site of present-day Montreal, where he encountered the powerful Haudenosaunee Confederacy, also known as the Iroquois. Despite initial tensions, Cartier managed to negotiate peaceful interactions with the Haudenosaunee and even took two sons of their leaders back to France.

In 1541, Cartier embarked on his third and final voyage, aiming to establish a French settlement in the newly claimed territory. He sailed up the St. Lawrence River, reaching a site near present-day Quebec City. Cartier named the area "Hochelaga," believed to be the site of the present-day city of Montreal. However, the settlement did not thrive, and Cartier's efforts to establish a permanent French presence were unsuccessful.

The French interest in North America persisted, leading to subsequent expeditions and the establishment of successful French settlements in the 17th century. Samuel de Champlain, who followed in Cartier's footsteps, founded Quebec in 1608, marking the beginning of New France. Other French settlements, such as Trois-Rivières and Montreal, soon followed, solidifying French control in the region.

The French approach to colonization differed from that of the English and Spanish. The French focused primarily on fur trade and establishing friendly alliances with Indigenous nations. They forged economic partnerships with Indigenous peoples, trading European goods for valuable furs, which became a lucrative industry. These trade relationships were often built on mutual respect and cooperation, allowing the French to maintain a foothold in the region.

French settlements, while not as numerous as those of the English colonies to the south, fostered a unique cultural blend. The French settlers, known as habitants, intermingled with Indigenous peoples and formed familial and trade connections. This cultural exchange led to the development of a distinct French-Canadian identity, marked by a combination of French, Indigenous, and Catholic influences.

However, the French presence in North America was not without challenges. Conflict arose between the French and other European powers, particularly the British, who sought to expand their territories and trade dominance. These conflicts, such as the Anglo-French Wars, ultimately resulted in the transfer of New France to British control under the Treaty of Paris in 1763.

The era of French exploration and settlement, embodied by Jacques Cartier's voyages, left a lasting impact on the history and cultural fabric of Canada. It laid the groundwork for subsequent European colonization, the fur trade economy, and the development of a unique French-Canadian identity. The interactions between the French and Indigenous peoples, characterized by trade, alliances, and cultural exchange, shaped the early foundations of Canada as a multicultural nation.

The British Dominion and the Seven Years' War

The period following the transfer of New France to British control in 1763 marked a significant chapter in the history of Canada. The British Dominion, as it came to be known, saw the consolidation of British influence and the reorganization of the colony's governance. This chapter explores the impact of the British Dominion and the pivotal events of the Seven Years' War that shaped Canada's destiny.

With the Treaty of Paris in 1763, France ceded its North American territories, including New France, to Britain. The British Empire now controlled a vast expanse of land, extending from the Atlantic to the Mississippi River. This transfer of power brought profound changes to the lives of the French settlers, as they adjusted to new rulers, laws, and cultural influences.

Under British rule, the colony of Canada underwent significant transformations. The British government sought to assert its authority and maintain order in the recently acquired territories. It established a new administrative framework, dividing the territory into two provinces: Quebec and East Florida. This reorganization aimed to govern the diverse population more effectively and promote British influence.

One of the major events during this period was the outbreak of the Seven Years' War (1756-1763), also known as the French and Indian War in North America. The conflict pitted the major European powers against each other, with

Britain and France as the primary contenders. The war had far-reaching consequences for Canada, as it became a battleground between the two colonial powers.

The Seven Years' War was fought on multiple fronts, including North America, Europe, the Caribbean, and India. In North America, the conflict centered around the strategic control of the continent and its valuable fur trade. Both the British and the French sought to secure alliances with Indigenous nations, as they played a crucial role in the fur trade and military engagements.

The British ultimately emerged victorious in the Seven Years' War. The pivotal battle of Quebec in 1759, led by General James Wolfe, resulted in the fall of Quebec City to British forces. The following year, the Battle of the Plains of Abraham solidified British control over New France, leading to the surrender of Montreal in 1760. The war formally ended with the signing of the Treaty of Paris in 1763.

The consequences of the Seven Years' War were significant for Canada. Through the Treaty of Paris, Britain gained control over the entirety of New France, including Quebec, and effectively became the dominant colonial power in North America. The French settlers faced a new reality under British rule, with changes in governance, legal systems, and language.

To address the concerns of the predominantly French-speaking population, the British government passed the Royal Proclamation of 1763. This proclamation recognized the rights and cultural practices of the French Canadians, allowing them to retain their language, religion (Catholicism), and civil law. It aimed to maintain social stability and prevent further conflict between the French and British populations.

The British Dominion also saw an influx of English-speaking settlers, known as United Empire Loyalists, who fled the American Revolutionary War and sought refuge in Canada. This migration further contributed to the growth of English-speaking communities and reinforced British influence in the region.

Despite the efforts to maintain social harmony, tensions between the French and British populations persisted. Language, cultural differences, and disagreements over land and governance created divisions within the colony. These tensions would eventually play a role in the rebellions and political struggles that emerged in the years to come.

The British Dominion and the outcome of the Seven Years' War set the stage for the future development of Canada. The British control over the territory would shape the formation of Canada as a distinct nation, with English and French cultural influences intertwined. It laid the groundwork for subsequent events, such as the American Revolution and the push for Canadian Confederation, which would further shape the destiny of this vast and diverse land.

The American Revolution's Impact on Canada

The American Revolution, a conflict fought between 1775 and 1783, had a significant impact on Canada, despite it being primarily centered in the Thirteen Colonies. This chapter explores the repercussions of the American Revolution on Canada and how the conflict influenced its political, social, and demographic landscape.

The American Revolution emerged from tensions between the American colonists and the British government, driven by grievances over taxation, representation, and the desire for greater self-governance. The revolutionaries aimed to secure independence from British rule, leading to a protracted and bitter conflict.

Canada, as a British colony, found itself in a precarious position during the American Revolution. The proximity of the Thirteen Colonies posed challenges and potential threats to British control over Canada. The revolutionaries sought to enlist support from the French-speaking population in Quebec, hoping to incite a rebellion against British rule.

The impact of the American Revolution on Canada can be examined through various lenses, including military, political, and demographic aspects.

Militarily, the conflict had direct implications for Canada's security. The revolutionaries, aiming to expand their territory and weaken British control, launched several military campaigns into Canada. The most notable of these was the invasion of Quebec in 1775 by American forces led by General Richard Montgomery and Colonel Benedict Arnold. Despite initial successes, the invasion ultimately failed, as the British and their Canadian allies successfully defended against the American advance.

The American Revolution also had political ramifications for Canada. The revolutionaries' ideals of liberty, self-governance, and republicanism resonated with some British colonists in Canada. These ideas fueled debates and discussions about the future of governance in Canada, with factions emerging advocating for greater autonomy and democratic reforms. However, these sentiments did not reach the critical mass necessary to spark a widespread rebellion, and Canada remained under British control.

One significant consequence of the American Revolution on Canada was the influx of United Empire Loyalists. Loyalists were individuals who remained loyal to the British Crown during the revolution and sought refuge in Canada following the American defeat. Thousands of Loyalists, including British officials, merchants, and settlers, migrated to Canada, bringing with them their cultural, political, and economic influence. This migration significantly impacted the demographics and development of Canada, particularly in areas such as Nova Scotia, New Brunswick, and Ontario.

The arrival of Loyalists also heightened tensions between the English-speaking Loyalists and the French-speaking population in Quebec. The Loyalists, with their English language and cultural background, added a new dynamic to the already complex linguistic and cultural landscape of Canada. Efforts were made to accommodate the Loyalists, such as the creation of separate Loyalist settlements and the division of Quebec into Upper and Lower Canada to address the concerns of the English-speaking population.

Economically, the American Revolution disrupted trade patterns and had consequences for Canada's economy. Prior to the revolution, the Thirteen Colonies were significant trading partners for Canada, providing valuable markets for Canadian goods. With the outbreak of the war, trade routes were disrupted, and Canada had to adapt to new economic realities. However, the loss of the American market also presented opportunities for Canada to develop new trading relationships, particularly with Britain and other British colonies.

While the American Revolution did not result in immediate political change or widespread rebellion in Canada, its impact was felt in various ways. The conflict highlighted the complexities of governance and cultural diversity within the colony. It brought demographic shifts with the arrival of Loyalists, contributing to the expansion of English-speaking communities and the multicultural fabric of Canada.

The American Revolution served as a backdrop to subsequent events in Canada's history, such as the push for Canadian Confederation in the mid-19th century. The ideals of liberty, self-governance, and constitutional rights that emerged during the revolution influenced political thought and the trajectory of Canada's own path to nationhood.

The War of 1812 and Its Consequences

The War of 1812, a conflict fought between the United States and Great Britain, had profound consequences for Canada. This chapter explores the causes, key events, and the lasting impact of the war on Canada's history, identity, and relationship with its neighbors.

The War of 1812 emerged from a combination of factors, including territorial disputes, trade restrictions, and the desire for national sovereignty. Tensions between the United States and Great Britain had been simmering since the American Revolution, and the issues surrounding maritime rights and impressment of American sailors further strained the relationship.

One significant cause of the war was the desire of some American expansionists to acquire more territory, particularly Canada, which was still under British control. The United States saw an opportunity to expand its borders and weaken British influence in North America.

The war unfolded with a series of military campaigns and engagements that occurred on both land and water. It began in 1812 when the United States declared war on Britain. American forces launched invasions into Upper Canada (now Ontario) in an attempt to capture territory and force the British to cede control.

The early stages of the war saw mixed outcomes for both sides. American forces achieved some victories, such as the capture of Detroit and the successful defense of Fort

McHenry in Baltimore, which inspired the writing of "The Star-Spangled Banner." However, the British and their Indigenous allies also achieved significant victories, including the capture of Fort Niagara and the successful defense of Upper Canada against American invasions.

Naval battles played a crucial role in the war, with several notable engagements taking place on the Great Lakes and the Atlantic coast. The Battle of Lake Erie in 1813, led by American Commodore Oliver Hazard Perry, resulted in a decisive American victory and secured control of Lake Erie. This victory enabled further American incursions into Upper Canada.

One of the most iconic events of the war was the British invasion of Washington, D.C., in 1814. British forces, including troops that had just returned from the Napoleonic Wars in Europe, captured and burned the White House and other key government buildings. This event, known as the Burning of Washington, was a significant blow to American morale but did not alter the ultimate outcome of the war.

The war came to an end with the signing of the Treaty of Ghent in December 1814. The treaty restored the pre-war status quo, with no territorial gains or losses for either side. Despite the lack of clear victory, the war had far-reaching consequences for Canada and its relationship with the United States.

One of the significant consequences of the War of 1812 was the strengthening of Canadian nationalism and identity. The successful defense against American invasions fostered a sense of pride and unity among Canadians. The war reinforced the idea of Canada as a distinct entity within

North America, separate from the United States and aligned with British interests.

The war also had a lasting impact on Indigenous peoples in the region. Indigenous nations played a crucial role in the conflict, often siding with the British in defense of their territories and alliances. However, the aftermath of the war saw the erosion of Indigenous lands and rights as British and American interests continued to encroach upon Indigenous territories.

The War of 1812 also had economic consequences for Canada. The disruption of trade routes and the British naval blockade limited Canadian access to American markets, leading to economic hardships. However, the war also spurred domestic manufacturing and industrial development in Canada as a means of achieving self-sufficiency and reducing reliance on American trade.

Perhaps one of the most significant outcomes of the war was the impact it had on Canada-U.S. relations. The conflict laid the foundation for a long-standing peaceful and mutually beneficial relationship between the two nations. It established the framework for the peaceful resolution of disputes through negotiation and diplomacy, setting the stage for increased cooperation and trade in the years to come.

The Fur Trade and the Hudson's Bay Company

The fur trade played a vital role in the early history of Canada, shaping its economy, culture, and relationships between Indigenous peoples and European settlers. Central to this trade was the Hudson's Bay Company, a dominant force in the fur industry. This chapter delves into the significance of the fur trade and the role of the Hudson's Bay Company in Canada's history.

The fur trade in Canada had its roots in the Indigenous peoples' long-established hunting and trapping practices. Prior to European contact, Indigenous nations had been engaged in trading furs among themselves for centuries, using them for clothing, shelter, and cultural practices. The fur trade with Europeans, however, brought about a significant expansion and transformation of this practice.

The fur trade flourished in the 17th and 18th centuries, as European demand for beaver pelts, prized for their softness and water-resistant qualities, soared. The beaver fur was highly sought-after for the manufacturing of fashionable hats in Europe. This demand fueled a robust trade network that spanned vast territories across North America, with the Canadian fur-bearing regions playing a prominent role.

The Hudson's Bay Company (HBC), founded in 1670, emerged as a dominant player in the fur trade. The company was granted a charter by King Charles II of England, giving it exclusive trading rights over a vast territory known as Rupert's Land, which encompassed much of present-day northern Canada and the western Hudson Bay region.

The HBC established trading posts, known as forts, throughout its vast territory. These forts served as centers of commerce and interaction between European traders and Indigenous peoples. The company engaged in direct trade with Indigenous nations, exchanging European goods such as textiles, tools, and metalware for furs. The HBC's ability to provide a consistent supply of trade goods, its relationships with Indigenous communities, and its extensive network of forts gave it a competitive edge in the fur trade.

The fur trade brought about significant changes in Indigenous societies. Indigenous nations became active participants in the trade, supplying furs and acting as intermediaries in the exchange process. This trade led to the emergence of new economic patterns and cultural practices among Indigenous peoples, as well as the integration of European goods into their material culture.

The relationship between the HBC and Indigenous peoples was complex and varied across different regions and time periods. Some Indigenous nations developed mutually beneficial relationships with the company, forging alliances and engaging in intermarriage with HBC employees. These alliances often served as a means of protection, access to European goods, and increased trade opportunities.

However, the fur trade also had negative consequences for Indigenous communities. The demand for furs, particularly beaver pelts, led to the depletion of animal populations in many regions. This ecological impact disrupted traditional hunting patterns and put strain on Indigenous communities that relied on the fur-bearing animals for sustenance and cultural practices.

The fur trade also had political ramifications. The HBC's extensive land holdings and influence in Rupert's Land gave it considerable control over vast territories. The company maintained a quasi-governmental role, administering justice, issuing its own currency (known as "made beaver"), and employing a private army of fur traders and Indigenous allies to protect its interests.

Over time, the fur trade declined as changing fashion trends, the depletion of fur-bearing animals, and shifts in global economic dynamics reduced the demand for furs. The HBC gradually transitioned its focus to other industries such as agriculture, shipping, and retail, adapting to the changing economic landscape.

The legacy of the fur trade and the Hudson's Bay Company is intertwined with Canada's history. The trade played a significant role in shaping the early relationships between European settlers and Indigenous peoples, fostering cultural exchange, economic interdependence, and conflicts over land and resources. The HBC's influence and economic power left a lasting imprint on Canada's development, contributing to the establishment of settlements, the growth of trade networks, and the expansion of British influence in the region.

Confederation and the Birth of Canada

Confederation, the political process that led to the birth of Canada as a nation, marks a significant turning point in the history of the country. This chapter explores the factors, negotiations, and events that culminated in the creation of Canada as a federal dominion in 1867.

By the mid-19th century, the British colonies in North America had reached a critical juncture. The Province of Canada (consisting of present-day Ontario and Quebec), along with New Brunswick and Nova Scotia, faced numerous challenges, including political deadlock, economic disparities, and concerns over defense and security.

The idea of uniting these colonies gained traction as a potential solution to the challenges they faced. The vision of Confederation sought to create a stronger political entity that could address shared concerns, promote economic development, and enhance defense capabilities.

The groundwork for Confederation began to take shape with the Charlottetown Conference in 1864. Representatives from the Province of Canada, New Brunswick, and Nova Scotia met to discuss the possibility of forming a federal union. This conference laid the foundation for further negotiations and the eventual creation of Canada.

Subsequent conferences, including the Quebec Conference in 1864 and the London Conference in 1866, refined the details of the proposed union. Key figures such as Sir John A. Macdonald, George Brown, and George-Étienne Cartier played instrumental roles in shaping the discussions and overcoming challenges to achieve a consensus.

The discussions during the conferences revolved around various issues, including the division of powers between the federal and provincial governments, representation, economic policies, and the protection of minority rights. The delegates worked towards finding a balance that would satisfy the interests and concerns of each colony involved.

One of the significant compromises that emerged from the negotiations was the adoption of a federal system of government. This meant that power would be shared between a central government responsible for national matters and provincial governments with authority over regional affairs. This federal structure aimed to accommodate the diverse interests and needs of the participating colonies.

On July 1, 1867, the Dominion of Canada was officially established through the enactment of the British North America Act, now known as the Constitution Act, 1867. This act united the Province of Canada (divided into Ontario and Quebec), New Brunswick, and Nova Scotia into a federal dominion under the British Crown.

The birth of Canada as a nation brought about a range of changes and opportunities. It allowed for the expansion of the dominion's territories through subsequent agreements and acquisitions, including the addition of provinces such as Manitoba (1870), British Columbia (1871), Prince Edward Island (1873), and the Northwest Territories (1870s-1880s).

Confederation also provided a framework for the inclusion of other regions into the dominion. The entry of provinces such as Alberta and Saskatchewan in 1905, Newfoundland in 1949, and the later creation of territories such as Nunavut in 1999 further shaped the geographic and political landscape of Canada.

The formation of Canada as a federal dominion had its challenges and complexities. Indigenous peoples, whose lands were encompassed within the dominion's borders, faced significant consequences. Treaties and agreements were negotiated, often with uneven outcomes, leading to the loss of land and a disruption of Indigenous ways of life.

Confederation also sparked debates and conflicts over the balance of powers between the federal and provincial governments, linguistic and cultural issues, and the representation of diverse populations within the dominion. These debates continue to shape Canadian politics and society to this day.

Nevertheless, Confederation set the stage for the growth and development of Canada as a nation. It established a framework for democratic governance, the protection of individual rights, and the evolution of Canadian identity. The unity and cooperation among the provinces and territories, combined with the flexibility of the federal system, have contributed to Canada's stability and its ability to navigate social, political, and economic challenges.

The Canadian Pacific Railway and Westward Expansion

The construction of the Canadian Pacific Railway (CPR) stands as a monumental feat in Canadian history, facilitating westward expansion, connecting distant regions, and shaping the economic and social landscape of the country. This chapter delves into the significance of the CPR and its impact on Canada's development.

The idea of a transcontinental railway had been contemplated since the early days of Confederation. The vision of linking the eastern provinces with the vast expanses of the west was seen as a means to strengthen national unity, promote settlement, and facilitate trade and transportation.

The CPR project gained momentum in the late 19th century, driven by economic considerations, geopolitical factors, and a desire to secure British Columbia's place within the Canadian federation. The province, isolated by vast mountain ranges and the Pacific Ocean, sought better transportation links to the east to spur economic growth and development.

The construction of the CPR was an immense undertaking that faced numerous challenges. The rugged terrain, including treacherous mountains, dense forests, and vast distances, presented significant obstacles. The project required extensive engineering expertise, the labor of thousands of workers, and substantial financial investments.

The CPR construction began in 1871, under the leadership of Sir John A. Macdonald's government. The railway progressed in sections, with different contractors responsible for various stretches of the route. The work involved the clearing of land, blasting through mountains, laying track, and constructing bridges, tunnels, and stations.

The project brought together diverse groups of workers, including European immigrants, Indigenous peoples, Chinese laborers, and others. The Chinese workers, in particular, made a significant contribution, enduring harsh conditions and facing discrimination while working on the railway's western section.

The completion of the CPR had far-reaching impacts on Canada. It opened up new opportunities for settlement and economic development, allowing for the exploitation of natural resources, such as timber, minerals, and agriculture, in the western regions. The railway facilitated the movement of people, goods, and ideas, connecting communities and fostering cultural exchange.

The CPR also played a crucial role in solidifying Canada's sovereignty and extending its influence across its vast territory. With the completion of the railway, Canada was better able to assert control over its western territories, promoting Canadian identity and reinforcing the sense of a unified nation.

The CPR's impact extended beyond economic and political realms. The railway brought about social transformations, as it facilitated the movement of settlers, entrepreneurs, and workers to the west. The growth of cities and towns along the railway route, such as Winnipeg, Calgary, and

Vancouver, contributed to the development of vibrant urban centers in the west.

The CPR's influence on Indigenous peoples varied. The railway often passed through traditional Indigenous lands, leading to the displacement of some communities and disruptions to their ways of life. However, the railway also provided economic opportunities and access to goods and services for some Indigenous peoples, while Indigenous workers made significant contributions to the construction efforts.

The completion of the CPR also had a profound impact on Canada's relationship with the British Empire and global trade. The railway provided a vital link for the transportation of goods between eastern Canada and the Pacific, opening up new markets and trade routes. It solidified Canada's role as a gateway to the Pacific and strengthened its ties to the British Empire and other nations.

The construction of the CPR was not without controversies and challenges. It faced financial difficulties, delays, and political debates. The government provided subsidies and land grants to support the project, which stirred debates about public investment and the relationship between the state and private enterprise.

Despite these challenges, the Canadian Pacific Railway stands as an enduring symbol of Canada's westward expansion and national ambition. The completion of the railway unified the country geographically and economically, leaving a lasting legacy in the form of improved transportation infrastructure, economic growth, and the integration of diverse regions into a cohesive nation.

The Klondike Gold Rush

The Klondike Gold Rush of the late 19th century stands as one of the most iconic episodes in Canadian history, capturing the imagination of people around the world and leaving a lasting impact on the development of the Yukon and the nation as a whole. This chapter explores the origins, excitement, challenges, and legacies of the Klondike Gold Rush.

The discovery of gold in the Klondike region of the Yukon in August 1896 sparked a frenzied rush of prospectors seeking fortune and adventure. The news of the gold strike spread rapidly, igniting a wave of excitement and prompting thousands of individuals from diverse backgrounds to make their way to the remote and treacherous territory.

The origins of the Klondike Gold Rush can be traced to the efforts of George Carmack, Skookum Jim, and Tagish Charlie, who made the initial discovery along the Klondike River. Their discovery set off a chain of events that would forever change the landscape and dynamics of the region.

News of the Klondike gold spread like wildfire, drawing prospectors from far and wide. People from different walks of life, including miners, adventurers, businessmen, and even journalists, flocked to the Yukon in search of gold. The promise of unimaginable wealth and the lure of the unknown attracted men and women from all corners of the globe.

The journey to the Klondike was an arduous and perilous one. Prospective gold seekers faced a daunting trek, navigating harsh terrain, freezing temperatures, and treacherous river currents. The most popular route, known as the Chilkoot Trail or the White Pass, presented immense challenges as prospectors hauled their supplies and equipment over steep mountain passes.

Once in the Klondike, the search for gold proved to be equally demanding. The gold-bearing creeks and rivers of the region were quickly staked and claimed, leading to intense competition and disputes among the prospectors. The arduous labor of digging, panning, and sluicing gravel for gold required patience, perseverance, and considerable physical exertion.

The conditions in the Klondike were harsh, with bitterly cold winters and short, frenzied summers. The isolated and remote nature of the region posed logistical challenges, as the demand for supplies and infrastructure far outstripped the available resources. As a result, prices for essential goods skyrocketed, and the provision of basic necessities was often inadequate.

The Klondike Gold Rush brought about significant social and economic changes. The sudden influx of people transformed the once sparsely populated region into a bustling hub of activity. The boomtown of Dawson City, situated at the heart of the Klondike, rapidly grew into a vibrant community, boasting saloons, hotels, banks, and a variety of businesses catering to the needs of the gold seekers.

The gold rush also had profound impacts on the Indigenous peoples of the region. The influx of newcomers disrupted traditional hunting and fishing practices, and Indigenous communities often faced discrimination and exploitation. However, some Indigenous individuals and groups also seized opportunities arising from the gold rush, working as guides, traders, or participating in the mining activities.

Despite the immense number of people who ventured to the Klondike in search of gold, the actual yield was relatively modest compared to the initial expectations. The vast majority of prospectors did not strike it rich, and only a small fraction of them found significant amounts of gold. Nonetheless, the lure of fortune and the stories of those who did strike it rich continued to captivate the popular imagination.

The legacy of the Klondike Gold Rush extends beyond the individual fortunes won or lost. The gold rush contributed to the development of infrastructure, such as roads, trails, and telegraph lines, which would facilitate further settlement and economic activity in the Yukon. The influx of people and resources also spurred the establishment of government institutions and regulations to govern the region.

The Klondike Gold Rush left its mark on Canadian culture and folklore. It inspired literary works, such as the poems of Robert Service and the writings of Jack London, which romanticized the harsh realities and the spirit of adventure associated with the gold rush. The image of the gold seeker with a pickaxe and gold pan became an enduring symbol of the quest for prosperity and the rugged spirit of the North.

The Boer War and Canadian Identity

The Boer War, fought from 1899 to 1902 between British forces and the Boer republics in South Africa, played a significant role in shaping Canadian identity and its evolving relationship with the British Empire. This chapter explores the impact of the Boer War on Canada's sense of nationhood, its military contributions, and the complexities of its loyalty to the British Empire.

At the time of the Boer War, Canada was still a relatively young nation, having achieved Confederation in 1867. Its identity was still closely tied to its British roots, and the war presented an opportunity for Canadians to demonstrate their loyalty to the Empire and assert their place on the global stage.

The outbreak of the Boer War saw an outpouring of support from many Canadians who volunteered to fight alongside British forces. These volunteers, primarily young men, were motivated by a range of factors, including a sense of duty, adventure, and a desire to prove themselves on the battlefield.

Canadian volunteers served in various capacities during the war. The most notable contribution came from the Canadian Mounted Rifles, a contingent of skilled horsemen who played a crucial role in the conflict. Canadian medical personnel, including doctors and nurses, also provided invaluable support in field hospitals and medical units.

The war presented Canadians with their first major overseas military engagement, and it had a profound impact on the country's emerging national identity. It provided an opportunity for Canadians to demonstrate their loyalty to the Empire and showcase their military capabilities. Canadians saw themselves as part of a larger British imperial project and believed that their contributions to the war effort would secure their place within the Empire.

However, the war also highlighted the complexities of Canadian identity. While many Canadians embraced their British heritage and supported the war effort, there were also those who questioned Canada's involvement in a conflict that was not directly related to its own defense. Debates arose regarding the nature of Canadian loyalty to the Empire and the extent to which Canadians should be involved in overseas conflicts.

The war also had repercussions for Canada's relationship with its French-speaking population. The majority of Canadian volunteers came from English-speaking communities, and some French Canadians expressed reservations about participating in a conflict seen as primarily benefiting British interests. These sentiments reflected the broader tensions and debates surrounding Canada's dual linguistic and cultural heritage.

The war itself was marked by brutal tactics and harsh conditions, including guerrilla warfare and the establishment of British concentration camps. These aspects of the conflict generated controversy and criticism, leading to debates and soul-searching within Canadian society about the moral implications of the war.

The end of the Boer War marked a significant moment for Canada's evolving identity. The sacrifices made by Canadian volunteers and the recognition they received for their contributions fostered a sense of national pride and self-confidence. Canada had proven itself on the world stage and gained respect as a capable military force.

The Boer War's impact extended beyond military matters. It contributed to Canada's growing sense of autonomy and the belief that it could assert its own interests within the British Empire. It also laid the groundwork for Canada's future participation in conflicts such as World War I, where Canadian forces would make even greater contributions.

The complexities surrounding the Boer War and its implications for Canadian identity continue to be debated and studied. The war raised questions about the nature of Canadian nationalism, the relationship between Canada and the British Empire, and the evolving role of Canada on the world stage.

Canada in World War I

World War I, fought from 1914 to 1918, had a profound impact on Canada and its place in the world. This chapter explores Canada's involvement in the war, the sacrifices made by its people, and the transformative effects the conflict had on the nation.

When war broke out in 1914, Canada, as a member of the British Empire, was automatically drawn into the conflict. The outbreak of war ignited a wave of patriotism and a strong desire among Canadians to contribute to the defense of the Empire and its values.

Canada's involvement in World War I was multifaceted. The nation sent thousands of soldiers to fight on the Western Front, including major battles such as Ypres, the Somme, Vimy Ridge, and Passchendaele. Canadian soldiers earned a reputation for their bravery, tenacity, and willingness to endure the hardships of trench warfare.

The war effort extended beyond the military sphere. Canadians on the home front rallied behind the cause, participating in various forms of support, such as fundraising, war bond drives, and volunteering for organizations like the Red Cross. Canadian industries also shifted their focus to support the war effort, producing weapons, munitions, and other supplies.

The impact of World War I on Canadian society was far-reaching. The war brought about significant social, economic, and political changes. The sacrifices made by

Canadians, the loss of lives, and the toll on families left a lasting mark on the nation's collective memory.

The experiences of Canadian soldiers during the war were varied. Many endured harsh conditions, faced the constant threat of enemy fire, and witnessed the horrors of trench warfare. Canadians fought alongside soldiers from other Allied nations, forging camaraderie and deepening their sense of shared purpose.

One of the most significant milestones in Canada's military history came with the Battle of Vimy Ridge in April 1917. Canadian troops successfully captured the heavily fortified German positions, marking a significant achievement for the Canadian Corps. The battle is often cited as a defining moment for Canada, symbolizing national unity, bravery, and military prowess.

The war had a profound impact on the nation's identity. It brought forth a sense of maturity and growing independence as Canada emerged as a distinct military force within the British Empire. The sacrifices made by Canadians on the battlefield and the contributions of the home front instilled a sense of national pride and a belief in Canada's ability to shape its own destiny.

The war also highlighted the diversity within the Canadian forces. Soldiers came from different regions, linguistic backgrounds, and cultural communities, forging a sense of national unity through shared experiences and sacrifices. Indigenous peoples also played a significant role in the war effort, with many volunteering to serve despite facing discrimination and challenges.

The war was not without controversies and challenges. The conscription crisis of 1917 sparked heated debates over mandatory military service. While conscription was eventually introduced, it deepened divisions within Canadian society, particularly between English and French Canadians.

The armistice in November 1918 brought an end to the fighting, but the war's impact continued to reverberate throughout Canada. The loss of over 61,000 Canadian lives in the conflict left a profound void in families and communities across the nation. The war's aftermath brought challenges of reintegration, physical and psychological trauma, and the need to honor and remember the sacrifices made.

Canada's role in World War I marked a turning point in its history. The war solidified Canada's place as a respected member of the international community and set the stage for its increased independence in foreign affairs. The experiences of World War I laid the foundation for Canada's future military contributions and shaped the nation's commitment to peacekeeping and international cooperation.

The Roaring Twenties and the Great Depression

The 1920s, often referred to as the Roaring Twenties, and the subsequent onset of the Great Depression in the 1930s marked a significant period of economic, social, and cultural transformation in Canada. This chapter explores the contrasting experiences of prosperity and hardship during these tumultuous decades.

The Roaring Twenties in Canada were characterized by a sense of optimism, cultural change, and economic growth. The end of World War I brought about a period of relative stability and an appetite for change. Technological advancements, such as the widespread adoption of electricity and the automobile, contributed to a growing consumer culture and new forms of leisure and entertainment.

Urbanization and industrialization accelerated during this time, with cities experiencing rapid growth. Montreal, Toronto, and Vancouver emerged as vibrant cultural and economic centers, attracting immigrants and fostering a cosmopolitan atmosphere. Jazz music, dance halls, and speakeasies became popular forms of entertainment, reflecting the influence of American trends and the loosening of social norms.

The 1920s also witnessed significant advancements in women's rights. Canadian women gained the right to vote federally in 1918, and the decade saw increased activism for women's suffrage and gender equality. The "Flapper" style, characterized by shorter skirts, bobbed hair, and a more liberated attitude, challenged traditional gender roles and norms.

While the 1920s brought prosperity to some, it was not an era of universal success. Agricultural communities faced challenges due to overproduction, falling crop prices, and the economic impact of World War I. Farmers struggled with debt and declining incomes, leading to economic hardships in rural areas.

The stock market crash of 1929 in the United States had far-reaching consequences for Canada. The subsequent onset of the Great Depression sent shockwaves throughout the global economy, severely impacting Canada's industries, businesses, and individuals. The country's heavy reliance on exports, particularly of primary resources, left it vulnerable to the collapse of international markets.

The Great Depression plunged Canada into a period of economic devastation, mass unemployment, and social upheaval. Industries faced closures, banks failed, and families struggled to make ends meet. The collapse of global trade led to a decline in commodity prices, further exacerbating the economic crisis.

The Canadian government implemented various measures to address the impact of the Great Depression. Prime Minister R.B. Bennett's administration introduced relief programs, such as the creation of public works projects and the implementation of unemployment insurance. However, these measures were limited in their reach and often insufficient to alleviate widespread suffering.

The Great Depression had a profound impact on Canadian society. Poverty and unemployment affected families across the country, leading to widespread hardships and the loss of homes and livelihoods. The era witnessed an increase in homelessness, breadlines, and the emergence of shantytowns, such as the "Forgotten Men" camps in major cities.

During this time, social and political movements gained traction as Canadians sought solutions to the crisis. The Co-operative Commonwealth Federation (CCF), a precursor to the modern-day New Democratic Party (NDP), advocated for social and economic reforms to address inequality and poverty. Labor movements also grew in strength as workers fought for better wages and working conditions.

The Great Depression had lasting effects on the Canadian economy and government policies. It prompted a reevaluation of the role of the state in ensuring economic stability and social welfare. The implementation of social safety net programs and the expansion of government intervention became part of the legacy of the Great Depression, shaping the development of Canada's welfare state.

Canada's experience of the Great Depression was not uniform across the country. Certain regions, such as the Prairie provinces, were particularly hard-hit due to their heavy reliance on agriculture. In contrast, resource-rich provinces like British Columbia benefited from increased demand for raw materials, albeit with fluctuating prices.

The end of the Great Depression was marked by the outbreak of World War II, which brought a renewed sense of economic activity and government investment. The war would once again reshape Canada's society, economy, and international role.

World War II and Canada's Role

World War II, fought from 1939 to 1945, had a profound impact on Canada and its role in the global stage. This chapter explores Canada's involvement in the war, its contributions to the Allied cause, and the transformative effects the conflict had on the nation.

When war broke out in 1939, Canada, as part of the British Commonwealth, declared war on Germany. The country quickly mobilized its resources and committed itself to supporting the Allied cause. The war effort demanded sacrifices from all segments of Canadian society, from the military to the home front.

Canada's military contribution during World War II was significant. Over one million Canadians, both men and women, served in uniform. The Canadian Army, Navy, and Air Force fought in major theaters of war, including Europe, the Atlantic, and the Pacific. Canadian troops played key roles in crucial battles, such as the Dieppe Raid, the Italian Campaign, and the liberation of the Netherlands.

The Royal Canadian Air Force (RCAF) played a vital role in the war's aerial campaigns. Canadian pilots flew with distinction in the Battle of Britain and other major air battles, while Canadian aircraft production supported the Allied air forces. The RCAF's No. 6 Bomber Group, stationed in England, contributed to the strategic bombing campaign against Germany.

Canada's naval forces played a crucial role in protecting vital shipping routes and supporting Allied operations. The

Royal Canadian Navy (RCN) contributed warships and personnel to convoy duty, anti-submarine warfare, and amphibious operations. The RCN's corvettes, known as the "Flower-class" corvettes, were renowned for their effectiveness in escorting convoys across the treacherous Atlantic.

In addition to its military contributions, Canada played a significant role in the home front war effort. The country's industrial production ramped up to support the war, with factories converting to wartime production. Canadian industries produced war materials, including weapons, ammunition, vehicles, and aircraft. The Canadian government implemented rationing and price controls to manage scarce resources and ensure equitable distribution.

Women's contributions during World War II were also crucial. With men serving in the military, women took on vital roles in the workforce, filling positions in factories, offices, and other essential sectors. The war effort challenged traditional gender roles and paved the way for increased gender equality in Canadian society.

The war had a profound impact on Canada's economy. Increased government spending and industrial production stimulated economic growth, leading to improved living standards for many Canadians. War-related industries provided employment opportunities and economic stability during a time of global upheaval. The war also prompted the development of new technologies and innovations, such as radar and atomic energy.

The internment of Japanese Canadians during World War II remains a dark chapter in Canadian history. In the wake of the Pearl Harbor attack and growing anti-Japanese sentiment, the Canadian government forcibly relocated Japanese Canadians from coastal areas and interned them in camps. The internment had devastating effects on the Japanese Canadian community, resulting in the loss of homes, businesses, and personal belongings.

Canada's involvement in World War II played a significant role in shaping the nation's identity and its place in the world. The war solidified Canada's status as a respected member of the Allied forces and strengthened its ties with the United States and other global powers. The experiences of Canadian soldiers and civilians during the war fostered a sense of national unity, resilience, and sacrifice.

The post-war period brought lasting changes to Canada. The country experienced a wave of immigration, particularly from war-torn Europe, which contributed to its cultural diversity and demographic transformation. The war also influenced Canada's foreign policy, as the nation actively participated in the establishment of the United Nations and pursued international cooperation and peacekeeping initiatives.

Post-War Canada: The Baby Boom and Economic Growth

The period following World War II marked a time of significant social, economic, and demographic changes in Canada. This chapter explores the impact of the post-war period, the phenomenon of the baby boom, and the subsequent economic growth that characterized the nation.

In the aftermath of World War II, Canada experienced a surge in population growth known as the baby boom. This demographic phenomenon was fueled by returning soldiers and their families, as well as a sense of optimism and a desire to rebuild after the war. The baby boom lasted from approximately 1946 to 1965, resulting in a significant increase in the number of births.

The baby boom had far-reaching effects on Canadian society. The rapid increase in the population created a surge in demand for goods, services, and housing, stimulating economic growth. Industries that catered to the needs of families, such as housing construction, baby products, and education, flourished during this period.

The post-war period also witnessed significant economic expansion in Canada. The country experienced sustained economic growth, driven by increased consumer demand, government investment in infrastructure, and the development of industries. Canada's natural resources, including forestry, mining, and oil, played a crucial role in driving economic development and attracting foreign investment.

Technological advancements further fueled economic growth. Industries such as manufacturing, telecommunications, and transportation benefited from innovations, leading to increased productivity and efficiency. The expansion of the automobile industry, for example, transformed mobility and contributed to the growth of suburban communities.

Government policies and initiatives played a significant role in fostering economic growth during the post-war period. The Canadian government implemented measures to support industrial development, including subsidies, tax incentives, and infrastructure investments. The development of social programs, such as universal healthcare (Medicare) and the Canada Pension Plan, also contributed to social stability and economic security.

The post-war period brought about changes in the labor market. The expansion of industries and the baby boom generation entering the workforce led to a significant demand for skilled workers. Immigration policies were adjusted to attract workers from abroad, contributing to the country's cultural diversity and enriching the labor force.

Suburbanization became a defining feature of the post-war period. As families sought affordable housing and space, suburbs grew rapidly around major cities. This shift in housing patterns, coupled with the expansion of transportation networks, transformed the urban landscape and led to the creation of new communities.

The post-war period also witnessed shifts in social attitudes and cultural expressions. The rise of consumer culture, fueled by economic prosperity, influenced lifestyles and aspirations. The emergence of popular culture, including music, film, and television, reflected the changing values and desires of the time.

The impact of the baby boom generation extended beyond demographic changes. As this generation reached adulthood, they became agents of social and political change. Their values and aspirations influenced various aspects of Canadian society, including education, civil rights, and environmental movements.

The post-war economic growth and the baby boom era had both positive and negative implications. The economic prosperity brought improved living standards for many Canadians, increased access to education and healthcare, and opportunities for upward mobility. However, economic disparities persisted, and certain groups, such as Indigenous peoples and marginalized communities, faced ongoing challenges and inequalities.

The Quiet Revolution in Quebec

The Quiet Revolution, also known as the Révolution tranquille, was a period of rapid social, cultural, and political change in Quebec during the 1960s. This chapter explores the factors that contributed to the Quiet Revolution, its impact on Quebec society, and its lasting legacies.

The Quiet Revolution emerged in the context of Quebec's evolving political and social landscape. For decades, Quebec had been characterized by conservative values, a dominant Catholic Church, and limited economic opportunities. However, by the mid-20th century, Quebec society began to undergo significant transformations.

Several factors contributed to the catalyst for change during the Quiet Revolution. First, a growing dissatisfaction with the traditional institutions, including the Catholic Church and conservative political elites, created a desire for social, cultural, and political renewal. Quebecers sought greater control over their own destiny and challenged the authority of established institutions.

Second, the rise of a more educated and urbanized population fueled demands for social equality, improved social services, and economic development. The baby boom generation, which came of age during this period, played a significant role in driving social and political change, as they sought greater opportunities and an end to the constraints of the past.

Third, the influence of global social and political movements, such as the civil rights movement and decolonization efforts, resonated with Quebecers who sought to challenge systemic inequalities and assert their cultural identity.

The Quiet Revolution encompassed a wide range of changes across various aspects of Quebec society. In the political sphere, the provincial government, led by Premier Jean Lesage and the Liberal Party, implemented a series of progressive reforms known as the "Lesage Revolution." These reforms aimed to modernize the province, redistribute wealth, and enhance social welfare.

Economically, the Quiet Revolution witnessed a shift toward a more interventionist government approach. The provincial government played a more active role in economic planning, invested in infrastructure projects, and encouraged industrialization and diversification. This approach aimed to reduce Quebec's economic dependence on traditional sectors, such as agriculture and resource extraction.

In the education sector, the Quiet Revolution brought about significant changes. The government implemented educational reforms, including the creation of the Ministry of Education, the expansion of public education, and the secularization of schools. These measures aimed to modernize the education system, promote French-language instruction, and reduce the influence of the Catholic Church in education.

The Quiet Revolution also had a profound impact on the cultural and linguistic dynamics of Quebec. The promotion of Quebec's distinct cultural identity and the defense of the

French language became central objectives. Efforts were made to strengthen and preserve the French language through language laws, the promotion of French culture, and the increased visibility of Quebec's artists, writers, and filmmakers.

The Catholic Church, which had long held a dominant position in Quebec society, underwent significant changes during the Quiet Revolution. The Church's influence and power were challenged, leading to a decline in its social and political control. As Quebec society became more secular, a new relationship between the state and the Church emerged.

The Quiet Revolution was not without its tensions and conflicts. The changes implemented by the government and the questioning of traditional values created divisions within Quebec society. The rise of nationalist sentiment and demands for greater autonomy also fueled debates over Quebec's place within the Canadian federation.

The Quiet Revolution had lasting legacies on Quebec society and its relationship with the rest of Canada. It paved the way for the emergence of a distinct Quebec identity, characterized by a strong sense of cultural pride, linguistic rights, and a desire for self-determination. The Quiet Revolution also contributed to the redefinition of federal-provincial relations in Canada and prompted constitutional discussions on the recognition of Quebec as a distinct society.

The Canadian Charter of Rights and Freedoms

The Canadian Charter of Rights and Freedoms, enacted in 1982, is a fundamental document that guarantees individual rights and freedoms within the Canadian legal framework. This chapter explores the origins, content, and impact of the Charter on Canadian society and its ongoing significance.

The origins of the Canadian Charter of Rights and Freedoms can be traced back to the constitutional discussions and negotiations that took place in the 1970s and early 1980s. The desire to entrench and protect individual rights and freedoms within the Canadian Constitution was a key motivation behind the creation of the Charter.

The Charter is a central component of the Constitution Act, 1982, which is an integral part of Canada's legal framework. It forms part of the country's supreme law, ensuring that the rights and freedoms outlined within it are protected and upheld by the government and the judicial system.

The Charter consists of several sections that guarantee a wide range of rights and freedoms to individuals. These include fundamental freedoms, such as freedom of speech, religion, assembly, and association. The Charter also protects democratic rights, such as the right to vote and the right to participate in political activities.

Equality rights are a crucial aspect of the Charter, ensuring that individuals are protected against discrimination based on characteristics such as race, gender, sexual orientation, and disability. The Charter also includes legal rights, such as the right to life, liberty, and security of the person, as well as the right to a fair trial.

The Charter's impact on Canadian society has been significant. It has played a central role in shaping the legal landscape and protecting the rights and freedoms of individuals. The Charter provides a framework for legal challenges and allows individuals to seek remedies when their rights have been violated.

One of the key features of the Charter is its ability to strike a balance between protecting individual rights and allowing for reasonable limits. The Charter includes a section known as the "reasonable limits clause" or the "limitation clause," which states that certain rights and freedoms may be limited if it can be justified in a free and democratic society.

The Charter has been the basis for numerous landmark legal cases that have shaped Canadian jurisprudence. It has played a crucial role in addressing issues of discrimination, upholding freedom of expression, protecting minority rights, and ensuring fair treatment within the criminal justice system.

The Charter has also fostered a culture of rights consciousness and awareness among Canadians. It has empowered individuals and groups to assert their rights and challenge discriminatory practices or laws. The Charter's influence extends beyond the courtroom, permeating various aspects of Canadian society, including education, public policy, and public discourse.

The Charter has contributed to a more inclusive and diverse society in Canada. It has been instrumental in recognizing and protecting the rights of marginalized communities, such as Indigenous peoples, racial and ethnic minorities, women, LGBTQ+ individuals, and persons with disabilities. These groups have used the Charter as a tool for advocacy and achieving greater equality and social justice.

The Charter's impact goes beyond domestic affairs. It has become an influential model for other countries grappling with constitutional reform and the protection of rights. Canada's commitment to human rights and the rule of law, as embodied in the Charter, has earned international recognition and admiration.

However, the Charter is not without its critics and challenges. Some argue that it can impede the ability of governments to enact certain policies or regulations in the interest of the broader society. Others question whether the Charter adequately addresses the needs and aspirations of all Canadians, particularly those in marginalized or vulnerable situations.

Aboriginal Rights and Land Claims

The issue of Aboriginal rights and land claims in Canada is a complex and multifaceted topic that spans centuries of history. This chapter explores the historical context, legal developments, and ongoing challenges surrounding Aboriginal rights and land claims in Canada.

The history of Indigenous peoples in Canada predates the arrival of European settlers by thousands of years. Indigenous peoples have diverse cultures, languages, and traditional territories that have shaped their identities and ways of life. Prior to European colonization, Indigenous nations occupied and governed their lands according to their own systems of governance and law.

The arrival of European explorers and settlers in the 15th and 16th centuries brought significant changes to the relationship between Indigenous peoples and the newcomers. European colonization resulted in the displacement of Indigenous communities, the imposition of colonial governance systems, and the erosion of Indigenous land rights and autonomy.

The assertion of Aboriginal rights and land claims is grounded in the historical treaties, agreements, and relationships established between Indigenous nations and the Crown (representing the British and later the Canadian government). Treaties were often negotiated to address land use, resource sharing, and peaceful coexistence between Indigenous nations and the newcomers.

However, the interpretation and implementation of these treaties have been a source of ongoing dispute and contention. Many Indigenous peoples argue that the treaties were meant to be a nation-to-nation relationship, guaranteeing their rights, including the right to self-governance and the right to occupy and use their traditional territories. They assert that the treaties should be interpreted and implemented in a way that respects their inherent rights and perspectives.

Over the years, legal developments have played a significant role in defining and advancing Aboriginal rights and land claims. In the landmark decision of Calder v. Attorney General of British Columbia (1973), the Supreme Court of Canada recognized the existence of Aboriginal title, which refers to the inherent right of Indigenous peoples to their traditional lands. This decision laid the foundation for future legal developments in the area of Aboriginal rights.

In 1982, the inclusion of Section 35 in the Canadian Constitution Act recognized and affirmed the existing Aboriginal and treaty rights of Indigenous peoples. Section 35 has since become a crucial tool for Indigenous peoples to assert their rights and seek legal remedies for past wrongs and ongoing infringements.

In response to these legal developments, a framework for negotiating comprehensive land claim agreements and self-government agreements was established. These agreements, negotiated between Indigenous nations and the federal and provincial governments, aim to address historical grievances, clarify land rights, provide compensation, and foster self-determination.

Land claim agreements have been reached with various Indigenous groups across Canada, leading to the establishment of modern treaties and self-governing Indigenous nations. These agreements have had significant impacts on Indigenous communities, including increased control over land and resources, the development of governance structures, and economic opportunities.

However, the process of negotiating land claims and achieving reconciliation between Indigenous peoples and the Canadian government is an ongoing challenge. Many land claims remain unresolved, and there are complex issues surrounding overlapping claims, the interpretation of historical treaties, and the differing perspectives on the nature and extent of Indigenous rights.

The recognition and protection of Aboriginal rights and land claims require a commitment to dialogue, negotiation, and a willingness to address historical injustices. The reconciliation process involves acknowledging and redressing past wrongs, fostering meaningful consultation and collaboration, and creating mechanisms for Indigenous self-governance and economic development.

Efforts are being made to implement a more collaborative and rights-based approach to land and resource management, such as the recognition of Indigenous jurisdiction and the requirement for free, prior, and informed consent. These initiatives aim to strike a balance between economic development and the protection of Indigenous rights and the environment.

The issue of Aboriginal rights and land claims is of national significance and has implications for all Canadians. Achieving reconciliation and a just resolution of land claims require ongoing efforts from governments, Indigenous peoples, and Canadian society as a whole. It is a complex and evolving process that seeks to honor the rights, cultures, and aspirations of Indigenous peoples while forging a more inclusive and equitable future for all.

The National Energy Program and the Oil Crisis

The National Energy Program (NEP) and the oil crisis of the 1970s were pivotal events in Canadian history, with significant implications for the country's energy sector, economy, and regional relations. This chapter explores the context, goals, controversies, and outcomes of the NEP and its connection to the global oil crisis.

The oil crisis of the 1970s was triggered by a series of events that disrupted the global oil market. In 1973, the Organization of Arab Petroleum Exporting Countries (OAPEC) imposed an oil embargo against countries supporting Israel in the Yom Kippur War. This led to a significant reduction in oil supply and a sharp increase in oil prices worldwide.

The impact of the oil crisis was felt globally, but it had profound effects on Canada, a country heavily reliant on oil imports. The sudden increase in oil prices created inflationary pressures, fuel shortages, and economic instability. Canada's dependence on foreign oil highlighted the vulnerability of its energy sector and underscored the need for greater energy self-sufficiency.

In response to the oil crisis and the desire to assert greater control over its energy resources, the Canadian government, led by Prime Minister Pierre Trudeau, introduced the National Energy Program in 1980. The NEP aimed to achieve energy self-sufficiency, reduce reliance on foreign oil, promote Canadian ownership and control of the energy sector, and ensure fairer pricing for Canadian consumers.

The NEP included various policy measures and initiatives. It introduced a system of price controls on domestic oil and natural gas, limiting price increases to protect consumers. It also implemented a system of export taxes on oil and gas to discourage excessive exports and ensure a stable domestic supply.

Another key aspect of the NEP was the creation of Petro-Canada, a national oil company. Petro-Canada was established to promote Canadian ownership and control of the oil industry, participate in resource development, and provide a stable and affordable energy supply to Canadians.

The NEP faced significant controversy and criticism, particularly from oil-producing provinces like Alberta. Critics argued that the program unfairly targeted Western Canada, where the majority of the country's oil reserves were located. They claimed that the NEP's policies, such as price controls and export taxes, stifled investment, discouraged exploration and production, and hindered the growth of the oil industry.

The NEP also created tensions between the federal government and the oil industry, as well as between different regions of Canada. Provinces like Alberta, which relied heavily on oil production, felt that the NEP undermined their economic interests and violated their jurisdictional rights over natural resources.

Despite its intended goals, the NEP did not fully achieve its desired outcomes. It faced challenges and obstacles, including the global oil market dynamics and opposition from key stakeholders. Over time, the NEP's policies were modified and eventually phased out in the 1980s.

The legacy of the NEP is complex and subject to differing interpretations. Supporters argue that it helped diversify Canada's energy sources, fostered domestic ownership, and stimulated investment in alternative energy sectors. They also contend that the NEP highlighted the need for energy conservation, environmental sustainability, and the long-term planning of energy resources.

Critics, on the other hand, argue that the NEP's policies had negative consequences, including stifled investment, job losses, and a loss of confidence in the Canadian energy sector. They contend that the NEP created a sense of economic and regional division, particularly between Western and Eastern Canada.

The NEP and the oil crisis of the 1970s remain significant events in Canada's energy history. They underscored the need for energy security, the challenges of balancing regional interests, and the complexities of energy policy in a global context. The experiences and lessons learned from the NEP continue to shape energy discussions, policy decisions, and debates surrounding Canada's energy future.

Canada-US Relations: NAFTA and Beyond

The relationship between Canada and the United States has been characterized by a unique blend of cooperation, interconnectedness, and occasional challenges. This chapter explores the historical context, the North American Free Trade Agreement (NAFTA), and the evolving dynamics of Canada-US relations.

The close proximity of Canada and the United States, sharing the longest international border in the world, has fostered extensive economic, cultural, and political ties between the two nations. The history of Canada-US relations dates back centuries, marked by periods of cooperation, trade, conflict, and negotiation.

In recent history, the signing of the North American Free Trade Agreement in 1994 was a significant milestone in Canada-US relations. NAFTA established a comprehensive trade agreement between Canada, the United States, and Mexico, aiming to eliminate barriers to trade and investment and promote economic integration in North America.

NAFTA had a profound impact on Canada-US trade and investment flows. It created a free trade zone that allowed for the movement of goods, services, and capital between the two countries with reduced tariffs and barriers. Canada and the United States became each other's largest trading partners, with billions of dollars' worth of goods and services exchanged annually.

The agreement facilitated the growth of integrated supply chains and the expansion of trade in various sectors, including manufacturing, agriculture, energy, and services. It also provided a framework for resolving trade disputes and protecting intellectual property rights, enhancing the predictability and stability of bilateral trade.

While NAFTA brought economic benefits, it also sparked debates and concerns on various fronts. Critics argued that the agreement had negative effects on certain industries and regions, leading to job losses and increased income inequality. They raised concerns about environmental standards, labor rights, and the potential erosion of national sovereignty.

The renegotiation of NAFTA, resulting in the United States-Mexico-Canada Agreement (USMCA) in 2020, reflected the evolving priorities and dynamics of Canada-US relations. The USMCA aimed to update and modernize the original agreement, addressing issues such as digital trade, labor rights, environmental protection, and intellectual property.

Canada-US relations extend beyond economic ties. The two countries collaborate on numerous issues, including defense, security, intelligence-sharing, environmental cooperation, and cultural exchanges. They have a long history of cooperation within multilateral frameworks, such as the United Nations, NATO, and the G7.

While Canada and the United States have a generally positive and cooperative relationship, there have been moments of tension and disagreement. Disputes have arisen over trade policies, border security, softwood lumber, agricultural products, and energy resources. However, the two nations have demonstrated a willingness to engage in dialogue and find diplomatic solutions to these challenges.

The personal rapport between Canadian and US leaders has often played a significant role in shaping the tone and direction of bilateral relations. Relationships between prime ministers and presidents have varied over time, ranging from close partnerships to more strained interactions.

The relationship between Canada and the United States is complex, multifaceted, and continuously evolving. It is influenced by a multitude of factors, including political dynamics, economic interests, cultural ties, and shared values. The two countries navigate their relationship with a combination of cooperation, negotiation, and the occasional disagreement.

Multiculturalism and Immigration

Multiculturalism and immigration have played significant roles in shaping the fabric of Canadian society. This chapter explores the historical context, policies, and the impact of multiculturalism and immigration on Canada's social, cultural, and economic landscape.

Canada is a nation built on immigration. Throughout its history, waves of immigrants from various parts of the world have contributed to the country's diversity and cultural richness. Indigenous peoples, as the original inhabitants of the land, have their own distinct cultures and histories that predate the arrival of European settlers.

The adoption of an official policy of multiculturalism in 1971 marked a significant turning point in Canadian society. Multiculturalism became a core value and a guiding principle of Canada's identity. The policy aimed to recognize, celebrate, and protect the cultural diversity of all Canadians, promoting inclusivity and fostering a sense of belonging.

Multiculturalism in Canada is grounded in the belief that cultural diversity is a source of strength, enriching the social fabric and contributing to the nation's development. It emphasizes the equal rights and opportunities of individuals, regardless of their cultural or ethnic background, and aims to create a society where all citizens can fully participate and contribute.

The policy of multiculturalism supports the right of individuals and communities to maintain and express their cultural identities, languages, traditions, and practices. It also encourages intercultural dialogue, understanding, and respect, fostering a sense of unity and shared values amidst diversity.

Immigration has been instrumental in shaping Canada's multicultural landscape. The country's immigration system is designed to attract skilled workers, entrepreneurs, family members of Canadian residents, and refugees, among others. Immigration policies have evolved over time, adapting to changing economic, social, and humanitarian needs.

The points-based immigration system, implemented in the late 1960s, prioritizes factors such as education, language proficiency, work experience, and adaptability. The system aims to select immigrants who are likely to contribute positively to Canada's economy and society. It also incorporates programs to reunite families and provide protection to those fleeing persecution or conflict.

Immigrants have made significant contributions to Canada's social and economic development. They have enriched the country's cultural tapestry, brought diverse perspectives and skills, and played a vital role in entrepreneurship, innovation, and job creation. Immigrants have contributed to various sectors, including healthcare, technology, education, arts, and sciences.

Integration and settlement programs support the successful integration of newcomers into Canadian society. These programs provide language training, employment assistance, access to education, and community support. They aim to facilitate newcomers' social and economic integration, helping them become active participants in their new communities.

Canada's approach to immigration and multiculturalism has not been without challenges. Some argue that the policy of multiculturalism can lead to cultural fragmentation and the formation of isolated communities. Critics also express concerns about issues such as social cohesion, economic competition, and strains on public resources. Debates and discussions surrounding these issues reflect the ongoing evolution of Canadian society.

As Canada continues to evolve as a multicultural nation, the importance of promoting social cohesion, addressing systemic barriers, and fostering inclusivity remains crucial. Efforts are being made to enhance the recognition and celebration of Indigenous cultures and languages, promote equity and diversity in all sectors, and address the unique needs of various ethnocultural communities.

The experiences of multiculturalism and immigration in Canada are dynamic and multifaceted. They reflect the ongoing evolution of Canadian society, the changing global context, and the commitment to building a diverse, inclusive, and welcoming nation.

Women's Rights and Feminism in Canada

Women's rights and feminism have been integral to Canada's social progress and the pursuit of gender equality. This chapter explores the historical milestones, key figures, and ongoing struggles in the quest for women's rights and the advancement of feminism in Canada.

The fight for women's rights in Canada has deep historical roots. In the late 19th and early 20th centuries, women began advocating for suffrage, seeking the right to vote and participate in the democratic process. After years of persistent activism, Canadian women achieved partial suffrage in 1916 and full suffrage in 1918.

The recognition of women's rights as human rights gained momentum in the mid-20th century. The United Nations' Universal Declaration of Human Rights, adopted in 1948, provided a global framework for the protection of women's rights and gender equality. Canada has been a signatory to numerous international conventions and treaties addressing women's rights.

The emergence of the feminist movement in Canada in the 1960s and 1970s brought attention to a wide range of women's issues, including reproductive rights, workplace equality, domestic violence, and gender discrimination. Feminist activists and organizations played a crucial role in raising awareness, advocating for policy changes, and challenging societal norms.

The Royal Commission on the Status of Women, established in 1967, played a pivotal role in shaping the feminist discourse in Canada. The commission's report, released in 1970, highlighted the systemic barriers faced by women and made recommendations for achieving gender equality in various spheres of Canadian society.

Legal reforms have been instrumental in advancing women's rights in Canada. The entrenchment of gender equality in the Canadian Charter of Rights and Freedoms in 1982 marked a significant milestone. The Charter guarantees equal rights and protections for all individuals, regardless of gender, and provides a legal framework for challenging discriminatory laws and practices.

Over the years, Canada has implemented legislation and policies to address gender-based discrimination and promote women's equality. These include laws to address pay equity, workplace harassment, reproductive rights, and access to childcare. However, ongoing efforts are required to address persistent inequalities and ensure the full realization of women's rights.

The advancement of women's representation and leadership roles in politics, business, and public life has been a key focus. Initiatives such as affirmative action and the implementation of quotas have aimed to increase women's participation and representation in decision-making positions. While progress has been made, there is still work to be done to achieve gender parity.

Violence against women has been a critical issue addressed by the women's rights movement. The establishment of shelters, support services, and legal protections for survivors of domestic violence and sexual assault has been a priority. Awareness campaigns and educational programs have also aimed to challenge societal attitudes and norms that perpetuate violence against women.

Intersectionality, recognizing the interconnected nature of discrimination based on gender, race, class, and other identities, has gained prominence within the feminist movement in Canada. This approach acknowledges the unique experiences and challenges faced by women from diverse backgrounds and strives for an inclusive and equitable feminism.

Women's rights and feminism continue to evolve in response to changing societal contexts and emerging issues. Indigenous women, women of color, LGBTQ+ individuals, and women with disabilities have contributed to the intersectional feminist discourse, advocating for recognition, representation, and justice.

Quebec Separatism and the Referendums

Quebec separatism and the referendums held in the province have been significant events in Canadian history, reflecting the aspirations, identity, and political dynamics of Quebec society. This chapter explores the historical context, key referendums, and the ongoing debates surrounding Quebec's relationship with the rest of Canada.

The roots of Quebec separatism can be traced back to the unique cultural and linguistic identity of the province. Quebec, with its predominantly French-speaking population, has sought to protect and preserve its distinct heritage within the broader Canadian federation.

The Quiet Revolution in the 1960s marked a period of significant social, cultural, and political transformation in Quebec. It fostered a sense of Quebecois nationalism, cultural affirmation, and demands for greater autonomy. The emergence of separatist sentiments was driven by a desire for self-determination and the belief that Quebec should be an independent nation.

The first referendum on Quebec sovereignty, known as the "1970 Sovereignty-Association Referendum," took place on May 20, 1980. The proposal presented to voters was for Quebec to negotiate a new political and economic relationship with Canada, based on the principles of sovereignty-association. However, the majority of Quebecers voted against the proposal, with approximately 60% opposing Quebec's secession.

The defeat of the 1980 referendum did not end the separatist movement in Quebec. Instead, it intensified debates and discussions surrounding Quebec's status within Canada. The federal government recognized the need to address Quebec's aspirations for greater autonomy and embarked on a process of constitutional reform.

The Constitution Act of 1982, which included the Canadian Charter of Rights and Freedoms, was a significant moment in Canadian history. However, Quebec did not fully endorse the constitutional amendments, and the province did not formally ratify the Constitution Act, highlighting ongoing tensions and disagreements.

The second Quebec referendum, often referred to as the "1995 Quebec Referendum," was held on October 30, 1995. The question posed to voters was whether Quebec should become a sovereign country. The result was a narrow defeat for the separatist side, with approximately 50.6% of Quebecers voting against sovereignty and 49.4% voting in favor.

The 1995 referendum sparked intense debates and raised important questions about the nature of Quebec's relationship with the rest of Canada. It also prompted the federal government to introduce legislation recognizing Quebec as a distinct society within Canada.

The referendums on Quebec sovereignty have had a profound impact on Canadian politics, the constitutional landscape, and the dynamics of intergovernmental relations. They have underscored the importance of dialogue, negotiation, and accommodation in addressing Quebec's aspirations while maintaining the unity of Canada.

While the referendums have drawn attention to the issue of Quebec separatism, it is essential to note that not all Quebecers support independence. Quebec's political landscape is diverse, with a range of viewpoints regarding the province's relationship with the rest of Canada.

The question of Quebec separatism remains a subject of ongoing debate and discussion. Many factors shape the dynamics, including linguistic, cultural, historical, economic, and political considerations. The aspirations and perspectives of Quebecers continue to evolve, influenced by changing societal dynamics and the broader Canadian context.

Canada's Healthcare System: Achievements and Challenges

Canada's healthcare system is a cornerstone of the nation's social fabric, providing universal access to essential medical services for all Canadian residents. This chapter explores the achievements, challenges, and ongoing debates surrounding Canada's healthcare system.

Canada's healthcare system is often referred to as a publicly funded, universal healthcare system. It is based on the principles of accessibility, comprehensiveness, portability, universality, and public administration. The system aims to ensure that all Canadians have access to necessary medical services regardless of their ability to pay.

One of the key achievements of Canada's healthcare system is the provision of medically necessary services, including physician visits, hospital care, and essential diagnostic tests, without direct charges to patients at the point of service. This universal coverage has helped to ensure that Canadians can receive the healthcare they need when they need it.

The establishment of the publicly funded healthcare system in Canada can be traced back to the introduction of provincial health insurance plans in the mid-20th century. The federal government played a role in facilitating the adoption of these plans through financial contributions and the enactment of legislation.

The Canada Health Act, enacted in 1984, is a federal law that sets out the principles and conditions for provincial and territorial healthcare coverage. It reinforces the principles of accessibility, comprehensiveness, universality, portability, and public administration. The Act also provides for federal transfers to the provinces and territories to support healthcare delivery.

Canada's healthcare system has achieved notable outcomes in terms of life expectancy, infant mortality rates, and the treatment of acute and chronic diseases. It has contributed to the overall health and well-being of Canadians, providing essential care and support in times of need.

The system is also known for its emphasis on primary care, with family physicians playing a crucial role as gatekeepers to other specialized services. Primary care physicians provide comprehensive, ongoing care, coordinate referrals to specialists, and play a key role in preventive healthcare.

However, Canada's healthcare system faces several challenges. One significant challenge is the issue of wait times for certain medical procedures and access to specialists. Due to factors such as an aging population, increasing demand for services, and limited healthcare resources, wait times for elective surgeries and specialist consultations can be lengthy in some cases.

Another challenge is the sustainability of the healthcare system in the face of rising healthcare costs. Healthcare expenditures continue to increase due to factors such as technological advancements, new treatments, and an aging population. Balancing the need for quality care with fiscal responsibility is an ongoing challenge for policymakers and healthcare providers.

There are also regional disparities in healthcare access and outcomes within Canada. Rural and remote communities may face unique challenges in terms of healthcare access, specialist availability, and healthcare infrastructure. Efforts are being made to address these disparities through initiatives such as telemedicine and targeted healthcare investments.

The role of private healthcare services within Canada's publicly funded system is another area of debate. While the core of the healthcare system is publicly funded, some Canadians may choose to purchase private health insurance to access additional services or reduce wait times for certain procedures. The balance between public and private healthcare services is a topic of ongoing discussion and varies across provinces and territories.

Addressing the healthcare needs of vulnerable populations, including Indigenous peoples, low-income individuals, and those with mental health challenges, is another area of focus. Ensuring equitable access to care and addressing social determinants of health are crucial to achieving health equity in Canada.

Efforts are being made to improve healthcare delivery through various initiatives, such as electronic health records, health information systems, and investments in digital health technologies. These advancements aim to enhance care coordination, reduce administrative burdens, and improve patient outcomes.

Environmentalism and Conservation Efforts

Environmentalism and conservation efforts have gained prominence in Canada and worldwide as concerns about the state of the natural environment and the impacts of human activities have grown. This chapter explores the historical context, key initiatives, and ongoing challenges in the realm of environmentalism and conservation in Canada.

Canada is known for its vast and diverse natural landscapes, including expansive forests, pristine lakes, rugged coastlines, and rich biodiversity. The recognition of the intrinsic value of the environment and the need to protect it has shaped the environmental movement in Canada.

Environmentalism in Canada has its roots in the conservation movements of the late 19th and early 20th centuries. Concerns about the exploitation of natural resources, such as timber and wildlife, led to the establishment of national parks, the protection of endangered species, and the promotion of sustainable resource management practices.

One of the notable achievements in environmental conservation in Canada is the creation of a network of national parks and protected areas. Parks Canada, established in 1911, has been instrumental in preserving and managing these protected areas, which encompass a diverse range of ecosystems and habitats.

The commitment to conservation and sustainable development is reflected in initiatives such as the Migratory Bird Convention, signed between Canada and the United States in 1916. This agreement aimed to protect migratory bird species and their habitats, highlighting the importance of international cooperation in environmental conservation.

In the 1960s and 1970s, the modern environmental movement gained momentum in Canada, influenced by global events and concerns such as pollution, deforestation, and the impacts of industrial development. Environmental organizations, grassroots activism, and public awareness campaigns emerged as powerful forces advocating for environmental protection.

The establishment of the Department of the Environment in 1971 signaled a growing recognition of the need for comprehensive environmental policies and regulations. The department's mandate included the conservation and protection of natural resources, pollution prevention, and environmental assessment.

Environmental impact assessment processes were introduced to evaluate the potential environmental effects of proposed projects. These assessments aim to ensure that development projects consider the environmental impacts and incorporate measures to mitigate any adverse effects.

The recognition of Indigenous rights and knowledge has become an integral part of environmentalism in Canada. Indigenous peoples have long-standing relationships with the land and hold valuable knowledge and practices for environmental stewardship. Collaborative partnerships with Indigenous communities are increasingly being fostered to integrate traditional ecological knowledge into conservation and resource management practices.

Canada has also made international commitments to environmental conservation. The country is a signatory to various global agreements and conventions, including the United Nations Framework Convention on Climate Change, the Convention on Biological Diversity, and the Paris Agreement. These agreements highlight Canada's commitment to addressing climate change, protecting biodiversity, and promoting sustainable development on a global scale.

Despite significant achievements, environmentalism and conservation efforts face ongoing challenges in Canada. Climate change, habitat loss, pollution, and resource extraction continue to exert pressures on ecosystems and natural resources. Balancing economic development with environmental sustainability remains a complex and evolving task.

Engaging in sustainable practices, transitioning to renewable energy sources, and implementing ecosystem-based management approaches are among the strategies employed to address environmental challenges. Collaborative efforts between government, industry, civil society, and Indigenous communities are crucial for achieving meaningful environmental outcomes.

Public awareness, education, and citizen engagement play vital roles in promoting environmental stewardship. Individuals, organizations, and communities across Canada actively participate in environmental initiatives, such as waste reduction, sustainable agriculture, and community-based conservation projects.

The Arctic: Challenges and Opportunities

The Arctic region, with its vast landscapes, unique ecosystems, and strategic significance, presents both challenges and opportunities for Canada and the international community. This chapter explores the complex dynamics, environmental concerns, economic potential, and geopolitical considerations associated with the Arctic.

The Arctic region encompasses the northernmost parts of Canada, Greenland (an autonomous territory of Denmark), Russia, Norway, and the United States (through Alaska). It is characterized by extreme cold, ice-covered waters, and a fragile ecosystem that supports diverse wildlife, including polar bears, whales, seals, and migratory birds.

Climate change has had a profound impact on the Arctic, leading to the melting of sea ice, changing weather patterns, and alterations in ecosystems. The shrinking ice cover has opened up new possibilities for navigation, resource exploration, and economic activities in the region.

One of the significant challenges facing the Arctic is the need for environmental protection. The fragile Arctic ecosystem is susceptible to the impacts of human activities, including pollution, habitat disturbance, and the introduction of invasive species. Conservation efforts are crucial to preserving the unique biodiversity and mitigating the ecological consequences of climate change.

The search for natural resources in the Arctic has generated economic opportunities and raised environmental concerns. The region is believed to hold vast reserves of oil, gas, minerals, and fish stocks. However, resource extraction in the Arctic poses risks to the environment, cultural heritage, and the livelihoods of Indigenous communities.

The Indigenous peoples of the Arctic, including the Inuit, Yupik, Sami, and others, have inhabited these lands for thousands of years and have developed a deep connection with the environment. Their traditional knowledge and practices contribute to sustainable resource management and inform decision-making processes in the region.

The opening of Arctic shipping routes, such as the Northwest Passage, presents new economic possibilities for international trade and transportation. Reduced sea ice coverage has the potential to decrease shipping distances between Europe and Asia, offering shorter transit times and potential cost savings. However, challenges related to navigation safety, infrastructure development, and environmental protection must be addressed.

The Arctic also holds scientific importance. Researchers from various disciplines study the region to better understand climate change, the impacts on marine and terrestrial ecosystems, and the effects on global weather patterns. Collaborative efforts among Arctic nations and the international scientific community are essential for advancing knowledge and developing sustainable management strategies.

Geopolitical considerations play a significant role in the Arctic. The region's strategic location and the potential for resource wealth have sparked interests among Arctic nations and other global powers. The governance and management of the Arctic require cooperation, diplomacy, and adherence to international agreements and legal frameworks, such as the United Nations Convention on the Law of the Sea.

The Arctic Council, an intergovernmental forum composed of Arctic states and Indigenous organizations, plays a vital role in promoting cooperation, environmental protection, and sustainable development in the region. It provides a platform for dialogue and collaboration on various issues, including environmental monitoring, search and rescue operations, and indigenous rights.

While the Arctic presents economic opportunities and strategic considerations, it is essential to balance these with environmental protection, sustainability, and the rights of Indigenous communities. The pursuit of responsible resource development, environmental stewardship, and respect for Indigenous knowledge and rights are key principles in Arctic governance.

Canada's National Parks and Natural Wonders

Canada is renowned for its breathtaking landscapes, pristine wilderness, and abundant natural wonders. This chapter explores the diverse national parks and awe-inspiring natural features that showcase the country's immense beauty and ecological significance.

Canada's national parks are protected areas managed by Parks Canada, with the aim of preserving and presenting the nation's natural and cultural heritage. These parks offer visitors opportunities for recreation, education, and appreciation of the country's remarkable landscapes.

Banff National Park, established in 1885, holds the distinction of being Canada's first national park and one of the oldest in the world. Nestled in the Canadian Rockies, it is renowned for its majestic mountains, turquoise lakes, and abundant wildlife. The iconic Lake Louise and the town of Banff are popular destinations within the park.

Jasper National Park, located adjacent to Banff, is another stunning natural gem. It boasts the Columbia Icefield, the largest icefield in the Canadian Rockies, and a diverse range of ecosystems, including alpine meadows, deep canyons, and powerful waterfalls. Wildlife sightings, including elk, bears, and mountain goats, are common in this park.

Glacier National Park, located in the province of British Columbia, is known for its rugged mountains, ancient glaciers, and challenging hiking trails. The park's Rogers

Pass offers a spectacular drive through towering peaks, and the Illecillewaet Glacier showcases the park's icy wonders.

Yoho National Park, also in British Columbia, is home to the awe-inspiring natural wonder known as Takakkaw Falls. This magnificent waterfall drops over 300 meters, making it one of the highest in Canada. The park also features stunning hiking trails, pristine lakes, and the Burgess Shale fossil site, renowned for its exceptional preservation of prehistoric marine life.

Gros Morne National Park, located in Newfoundland and Labrador, is a UNESCO World Heritage Site known for its unique geological features. The park's Tablelands, a striking landscape of exposed earth's mantle, offer a glimpse into the Earth's ancient history. Hiking enthusiasts can explore the challenging Long Range Mountains, while coastal areas provide opportunities for whale watching and seabird spotting.

Cape Breton Highlands National Park, situated on the northern tip of Nova Scotia's Cape Breton Island, offers a remarkable fusion of rugged coastal cliffs, lush forests, and sweeping panoramic views. The park's Cabot Trail is a world-renowned scenic drive, showcasing the natural beauty of the region.

Nahanni National Park Reserve, located in the Northwest Territories, is a UNESCO World Heritage Site known for its deep canyons, stunning waterfalls, and the breathtaking South Nahanni River. This remote wilderness area offers opportunities for wilderness camping, paddling, and exploring the raw beauty of Canada's northern landscape.

Canada's national parks also encompass marine environments, such as Pacific Rim National Park Reserve on Vancouver Island. This park showcases the beauty of the rugged Pacific coastline, ancient rainforests, and rich biodiversity. Visitors can explore sandy beaches, hike through old-growth forests, and witness the power of the Pacific Ocean.

Beyond the national parks, Canada boasts numerous natural wonders that captivate visitors. Niagara Falls, located on the border between Ontario and New York, is one of the most famous waterfalls in the world, renowned for its thunderous cascade and mesmerizing beauty.

The Bay of Fundy, stretching between New Brunswick and Nova Scotia, boasts the highest tides in the world. Twice a day, billions of tons of seawater rush in and out, creating dramatic changes in coastal landscapes and providing a unique habitat for marine life.

Canada's natural wonders are not limited to specific parks or regions. From the stunning turquoise waters of Moraine Lake in Banff National Park to the majestic fjords of the Saguenay-St. Lawrence Marine Park in Quebec, the country's diverse landscapes offer a multitude of natural treasures to explore.

These national parks and natural wonders serve as reminders of the importance of conservation and the need to protect the fragile ecosystems that make Canada a haven for biodiversity. They offer opportunities for outdoor recreation, wildlife observation, and spiritual connection with nature.

Canadian Cuisine: From Poutine to Nanaimo Bars

Canadian cuisine is a diverse and eclectic reflection of the country's multicultural heritage, regional influences, and the availability of local ingredients. This chapter explores the unique dishes, culinary traditions, and iconic treats that contribute to Canada's gastronomic tapestry.

One of the most recognized and beloved Canadian dishes is poutine. Originating in Quebec, poutine consists of crispy French fries topped with cheese curds and smothered in rich gravy. This indulgent comfort food has gained popularity across the country and has even been reimagined with creative variations, including toppings like pulled pork, bacon, or even lobster.

Another Canadian favorite is butter tarts. These delectable pastries feature a sweet filling made from butter, sugar, and eggs, often with the addition of raisins or pecans. Butter tarts have become a quintessential Canadian dessert, enjoyed during holidays and year-round.

Nanaimo bars are a classic Canadian treat named after the city of Nanaimo in British Columbia. These no-bake squares consist of a buttery graham cracker crust, a custard-like middle layer, and a glossy chocolate ganache on top. Nanaimo bars are rich and satisfying, often making appearances at potlucks, bake sales, and family gatherings.

Maple syrup holds a special place in Canadian cuisine. Canada is one of the world's leading producers of maple syrup, harvested from the sap of maple trees. The golden, sweet syrup is not only a popular topping for pancakes and waffles but also used in a variety of recipes, from marinades and glazes to desserts and cocktails.

Tourtière is a savory meat pie traditionally associated with French-Canadian cuisine. This hearty pie is typically filled with a mixture of ground meat, such as pork, beef, or veal, seasoned with herbs and spices. Tourtière is often enjoyed during festive occasions, particularly around the Christmas season.

Regional specialties also play a significant role in Canadian cuisine. In Atlantic Canada, seafood takes center stage, with dishes like lobster rolls in Nova Scotia and seafood chowder in Newfoundland and Labrador. In the Prairie provinces, hearty meals like bison burgers and Saskatoon berry pies showcase the region's agricultural abundance.

Indigenous cuisine has a profound influence on Canadian culinary traditions. Traditional Indigenous foods include bannock, a type of bread cooked over an open fire, and pemmican, a mixture of dried meat and fat. These ingredients, along with wild game, fish, and foraged plants, contribute to a rich and diverse Indigenous food culture.

Canada's multiculturalism is reflected in its culinary landscape, with diverse ethnic cuisines thriving in cities and towns across the country. Chinese, Indian, Italian, Greek, and Middle Eastern foods, among many others, have become integral parts of the Canadian culinary scene, offering a wide array of flavors and dining experiences.

In recent years, there has been a growing emphasis on local, sustainable, and farm-to-table dining experiences. Canadian chefs and food artisans are championing the use of locally sourced ingredients, supporting local farmers, and promoting culinary creativity with a focus on seasonality and freshness.

Craft beer and wine production have also gained prominence in Canada. Microbreweries and wineries have flourished, producing a wide range of artisanal beers, ciders, and wines that showcase the country's unique terroir and craftsmanship.

Exploring Canada: From the Rockies to the Maritimes

Canada's vast and diverse landscapes offer a wealth of natural beauty and cultural experiences for visitors to explore. From the majestic Rocky Mountains to the charming coastal towns of the Maritimes, this chapter takes you on a journey across Canada's stunning regions.

The Rocky Mountains, located in western Canada, are a major draw for nature enthusiasts and adventure seekers. Banff National Park and Jasper National Park, nestled within the Rockies, offer awe-inspiring vistas of towering peaks, turquoise lakes, and abundant wildlife. Hiking, mountain biking, skiing, and wildlife watching are popular activities in this rugged and picturesque region.

Heading westward, the province of British Columbia showcases a stunning blend of mountains, forests, and coastline. The vibrant city of Vancouver, surrounded by the Pacific Ocean and coastal mountains, offers a vibrant urban experience along with easy access to outdoor adventures. Vancouver Island, just a short ferry ride away, boasts old-growth rainforests, rugged shorelines, and charming communities like Victoria and Tofino.

Continuing eastward, the Canadian Prairies unfold, characterized by vast expanses of flat plains and big skies. The province of Alberta is home to the awe-inspiring Badlands, where the unique rock formations of Drumheller and Dinosaur Provincial Park provide glimpses into the prehistoric world. The vast fields of canola, wheat, and other crops create a distinct rural beauty that stretches as far as the eye can see.

Crossing into the province of Saskatchewan, the prairies continue their vast embrace. The Grasslands National Park showcases the region's unique ecosystem, featuring rolling hills, native grasses, and an array of wildlife. Visitors can explore hiking trails, witness breathtaking sunsets, and experience the tranquility of this untouched landscape.

Further east, the province of Manitoba offers a blend of natural wonders and cultural experiences. The capital city of Winnipeg is a vibrant cultural hub, boasting museums, art galleries, and a thriving culinary scene. Outdoor enthusiasts can explore the vast boreal forests, pristine lakes, and catch a glimpse of polar bears in Churchill, known as the "Polar Bear Capital of the World."

As we venture eastward, we reach the province of Ontario, home to iconic destinations like Toronto, Niagara Falls, and the Great Lakes. Toronto, Canada's largest city, offers a diverse mix of cultures, world-class cuisine, and vibrant neighborhoods. Niagara Falls, a natural wonder shared with the United States, captivates visitors with its powerful cascades and mesmerizing beauty. The Great Lakes, including Lake Ontario and Lake Superior, provide opportunities for boating, fishing, and exploring charming waterfront towns.

Continuing east, we arrive in the province of Quebec, where the city of Montreal showcases a blend of European charm and North American flair. Old Montreal's cobblestone streets, historic architecture, and vibrant festivals create a unique ambiance. Quebec City, the provincial capital, offers a glimpse into Canada's rich history with its well-preserved fortifications and charming Old Town, designated as a UNESCO World Heritage site.

The Atlantic region, known as the Maritimes, includes the provinces of New Brunswick, Prince Edward Island (PEI), and Nova Scotia. Here, visitors can experience rugged coastlines, charming fishing villages, and warm Maritime hospitality. The Bay of Fundy, famous for its highest tides in the world, showcases breathtaking coastal scenery and provides opportunities for whale watching and tidal exploration. PEI, known for its red sand beaches, rolling farmland, and Anne of Green Gables heritage, offers a serene escape. Nova Scotia delights with its picturesque lighthouses, stunning Cabot Trail, and vibrant cultural scene centered around the historic city of Halifax.

Niagara Falls and Other Iconic Landmarks

Niagara Falls stands as one of the world's most renowned natural wonders, captivating visitors with its sheer power and breathtaking beauty. This chapter explores the awe-inspiring allure of Niagara Falls and delves into other iconic landmarks across Canada that have become symbols of the nation's natural and cultural heritage.

Niagara Falls, located on the border between Ontario, Canada, and New York, United States, consists of three waterfalls: the Horseshoe Falls, the American Falls, and the Bridal Veil Falls. The falls are formed by the mighty Niagara River, which connects Lake Erie to Lake Ontario. The thunderous cascade of water, combined with the mist and the rainbows that often grace the site, creates an unforgettable spectacle.

Visitors to Niagara Falls can experience the grandeur of the falls from various vantage points. The Canadian side, known as the Horseshoe Falls, offers unobstructed views of the massive horseshoe-shaped cascade. The American side provides close-up encounters with the falls and opportunities for scenic walks along the Niagara Gorge.

Beyond Niagara Falls, Canada is home to a host of other iconic landmarks that showcase the country's natural and cultural heritage. These landmarks have become enduring symbols of Canada and draw visitors from around the world.

The CN Tower in Toronto is one such iconic landmark, dominating the city's skyline. Standing at a height of 553.33 meters (1,815 feet and 5 inches), it held the title of the world's tallest freestanding structure for over three decades. The CN Tower offers panoramic views of the city and beyond, as well as thrilling experiences like the EdgeWalk, where visitors can walk along the tower's outer edge.

In Ottawa, the Parliament Hill complex is an iconic symbol of Canadian governance and democracy. The Parliament Buildings, with their stunning Gothic Revival architecture, overlook the Ottawa River and serve as the seat of Canada's federal government. Visitors can explore the grounds, take guided tours of the buildings, and witness the Changing of the Guard ceremony during the summer months.

Moving to the East Coast, the historic site of Peggy's Cove in Nova Scotia captivates visitors with its picturesque lighthouse and rugged coastal beauty. Perched on granite rocks against the backdrop of the Atlantic Ocean, Peggy's Cove has become an iconic representation of Maritime Canada, attracting photographers and nature enthusiasts alike.

In Alberta, the majestic Canadian Rockies are a magnet for outdoor adventurers and nature lovers. Iconic landmarks like Lake Louise, Moraine Lake, and the Columbia Icefield showcase the region's pristine wilderness, towering peaks, and turquoise glacial waters. These landmarks have become symbols of Canada's natural beauty and are often featured in travel magazines and postcards.

On the West Coast, the city of Vancouver boasts the iconic Stanley Park. This urban oasis offers a lush green escape with scenic walking trails, beautiful gardens, and the iconic seawall that winds along the waterfront. The park's Totem Poles, showcasing Indigenous art and culture, add a distinctive touch to this beloved landmark.

Indigenous cultural landmarks, such as the UNESCO World Heritage Site of Head-Smashed-In Buffalo Jump in Alberta or the ancient rock carvings of Writing-on-Stone Provincial Park in Alberta, provide insights into the rich history and traditions of Canada's Indigenous peoples.

These iconic landmarks, be they natural wonders, architectural marvels, or cultural sites, represent the diverse tapestry of Canada's heritage. They serve as reminders of the country's natural beauty, cultural richness, and historical significance.

Vancouver: A Vibrant City on the West Coast

Nestled between the mountains and the Pacific Ocean, Vancouver stands as a vibrant and cosmopolitan city on Canada's West Coast. This chapter explores the allure of Vancouver, highlighting its diverse culture, stunning natural surroundings, and thriving urban atmosphere.

Vancouver, the largest city in British Columbia, offers a unique blend of natural beauty, cultural diversity, and a mild climate that attracts residents and visitors alike. Surrounded by mountains, including the iconic North Shore Mountains, and bordered by the Strait of Georgia, the city is known for its picturesque landscapes and breathtaking views.

The city's downtown core is a bustling hub of activity, with a skyline dominated by modern high-rise buildings. The financial district, centered around Burrard Street, is home to numerous corporate offices and financial institutions. Vancouver's downtown also boasts a vibrant shopping scene, with popular destinations like Robson Street offering a mix of high-end boutiques and international brands.

One of Vancouver's most famous attractions is Stanley Park, a 400-hectare (1,000-acre) urban oasis located at the city's western edge. The park features lush forests, scenic walking and cycling paths, and stunning views of the city skyline and the North Shore Mountains. Within the park, the Vancouver Aquarium showcases a diverse array of marine life and offers educational programs for visitors of all ages.

Granville Island, located in the heart of the city, is a cultural hotspot that draws both locals and tourists. The Granville Island Public Market is a food lover's paradise, offering a wide variety of fresh produce, seafood, artisanal products, and international cuisine. The island is also home to theaters, art galleries, and a thriving artist community, making it a vibrant hub for arts and entertainment.

Vancouver's cultural diversity is evident in its vibrant neighborhoods. The historic Gastown district, with its cobblestone streets and Victorian architecture, is a popular destination for shopping, dining, and exploring art galleries. Commercial Drive, known locally as "The Drive," is a lively neighborhood filled with multicultural restaurants, trendy boutiques, and a bohemian atmosphere.

The city's culinary scene reflects its multicultural fabric, with a wide array of international cuisines to tantalize the taste buds. From sushi to dim sum, from farm-to-table bistros to food trucks, Vancouver offers a diverse range of culinary experiences. The city's proximity to the ocean ensures an abundance of fresh seafood, while its thriving craft beer and wine scene adds to the gastronomic delight.

Vancouver is also celebrated for its outdoor recreational opportunities. The surrounding mountains provide ample opportunities for hiking, skiing, snowboarding, and mountain biking. Grouse Mountain, Cypress Mountain, and Mount Seymour are popular destinations for outdoor enthusiasts seeking adventure and breathtaking vistas.

For those seeking a beach experience, Vancouver's shoreline offers picturesque spots such as English Bay, Kitsilano Beach, and Jericho Beach. These sandy stretches are perfect for sunbathing, picnicking, and enjoying stunning sunsets over the Pacific Ocean.

Vancouver's commitment to sustainability and green initiatives is evident throughout the city. Biking infrastructure, electric vehicle charging stations, and a comprehensive public transit system make it easy to explore the city and minimize environmental impact. The city's dedication to preserving its natural surroundings is also reflected in the many parks, gardens, and green spaces scattered throughout its neighborhoods.

In addition to its natural and cultural attractions, Vancouver hosts a variety of festivals and events throughout the year. The Vancouver International Film Festival, the Celebration of Light fireworks competition, and the Vancouver Folk Music Festival are just a few examples of the city's vibrant arts and entertainment scene.

Ottawa: The Capital City and Its Historic Sites

Ottawa, the capital city of Canada, holds a significant place in the nation's history and serves as a symbol of Canadian governance and democracy. This chapter explores the allure of Ottawa, highlighting its historic sites, cultural landmarks, and the unique blend of heritage and modernity that defines the city.

Situated in the eastern part of the province of Ontario, Ottawa is located at the confluence of the Ottawa, Gatineau, and Rideau Rivers. Its strategic location on the border of Ontario and Quebec has played a pivotal role in shaping the city's identity and cultural fabric.

The Parliament Hill complex stands as the heart of Ottawa and the focal point of Canada's federal government. The iconic Parliament Buildings, with their Gothic Revival architecture, dominate the city's skyline. Centered around the Peace Tower, the buildings house the House of Commons, the Senate, and other administrative offices. Visitors can take guided tours of the Parliament Buildings and learn about Canada's political system and history.

Adjacent to Parliament Hill, the historic Rideau Canal adds charm and character to the city. This UNESCO World Heritage Site stretches over 202 kilometers (126 miles) and connects Ottawa to Lake Ontario. During the winter months, the canal transforms into the world's largest skating rink, providing a unique and cherished experience for locals and visitors alike.

The National Gallery of Canada, located near Parliament Hill, showcases an extensive collection of Canadian and international art. Its striking glass and granite structure houses masterpieces, including works by the Group of Seven, Emily Carr, and other renowned artists. The gallery's architecture itself is a work of art, with sweeping views of the Ottawa River and the cityscape.

The Canadian Museum of History, situated just across the Ottawa River in Gatineau, Quebec, provides insight into Canada's rich history and cultural heritage. The museum's exhibitions delve into the nation's Indigenous past, European exploration and settlement, and the diverse contributions of different communities that have shaped the country.

The ByWard Market, one of Canada's oldest public markets, is a vibrant hub of activity in downtown Ottawa. Dating back to the early 19th century, the market offers a delightful mix of fresh produce, artisanal products, specialty foods, and boutiques. It is also a lively area for dining and entertainment, with an array of restaurants, cafes, and nightlife options.

Just a short distance from the city center, the Rideau Hall serves as the official residence of the Governor General of Canada. This historic site showcases beautiful grounds and gardens, and it plays a significant role in ceremonial and diplomatic events.

Ottawa's heritage is also preserved in its many historic neighborhoods, such as the charming and picturesque area of ByWard Market, Sandy Hill, and the Glebe. These neighborhoods feature beautifully preserved Victorian and

Edwardian architecture, boutique shops, cozy cafes, and tree-lined streets.

The National War Memorial, located near Parliament Hill, honors the Canadian soldiers who have fought and sacrificed in various conflicts. This iconic landmark is the site of annual Remembrance Day ceremonies and serves as a place of reflection and tribute.

As the capital city, Ottawa also hosts a range of cultural festivals and events throughout the year. Winterlude, a celebration of winter and ice sculpture, showcases the beauty and fun of the Canadian winter. The Canadian Tulip Festival, held in spring, displays stunning floral displays and celebrates the gift of tulips from the Netherlands as a symbol of friendship.

Ottawa's commitment to green spaces and natural beauty is evident in its numerous parks and gardens. Major parks, including Major's Hill Park and Confederation Park, provide green oases for relaxation and outdoor activities in the heart of the city. The Rideau Falls, where the Rideau River meets the Ottawa River, offers a scenic spot to appreciate the power and beauty of nature.

Ottawa's cultural diversity is also reflected in its vibrant culinary scene. The city boasts a wide range of international cuisines, from French and Italian to Middle Eastern and Asian, with diverse dining options to suit every palate and budget.

Conclusion

Throughout this book, we have embarked on a journey through the history, culture, and landmarks of Canada. From its Indigenous roots to its colonial past, from the confederation that birthed the nation to the challenges and triumphs of modern times, Canada has evolved into a diverse and resilient country.

We have explored Canada's vast landscapes, from the rugged Rocky Mountains to the picturesque coastlines of the Maritimes. We have marveled at the natural wonders, such as Niagara Falls and the Canadian Rockies, that attract visitors from around the world. We have delved into the vibrant cities, like Vancouver and Ottawa, that blend history and modernity, offering unique experiences and cultural treasures.

Canada's multiculturalism has been a constant thread in our exploration. The country's history is enriched by the contributions of Indigenous peoples, European settlers, and immigrants from around the globe. This diversity is reflected in Canada's cuisine, its artistic expressions, and its rich tapestry of cultural traditions.

From the early explorers seeking new trade routes to the conflicts that shaped the nation, Canada's history is marked by both triumphs and challenges. The struggles for Indigenous rights, women's rights, and social equality have shaped the country's identity and continue to inspire ongoing progress.

Canada's commitment to social welfare is exemplified by its healthcare system, which provides universal access to medical care. The country's education system, its emphasis on human rights and freedoms, and its dedication to environmental sustainability reflect a national ethos of inclusivity and responsibility.

As we conclude this journey, we recognize that Canada is a country that embraces its past while looking to the future. Its natural beauty, diverse cultural mosaic, and commitment to social progress make it a unique and remarkable nation.

From the ancient history of the Indigenous peoples to the modern achievements and challenges, Canada's story is one of resilience, innovation, and an ongoing quest for harmony. The country's people, its landscapes, and its vibrant cities all contribute to the tapestry that is Canada.

As we close this book, may it serve as an invitation to further explore the wonders of Canada, to deepen our understanding of its history, and to appreciate the richness of its cultural heritage. Canada is a country that continues to evolve, and its story is an ongoing narrative of discovery, unity, and shared aspirations.

May we carry the spirit of exploration, understanding, and respect for Canada and its people as we embark on our own journeys, both within its borders and beyond. Canada's history and its place in the world offer lessons, inspiration, and a profound appreciation for the beauty and diversity of our global community.

Thank you for embarking on this journey through the history of Canada with me. I hope that this book has provided you with valuable insights, fascinating facts, and a deeper appreciation for the rich tapestry of Canada's past and present.

Your support as a reader means a great deal to me, and I would be grateful if you could take a moment to leave a positive review of this book. Your feedback and endorsement will not only encourage others to discover the wonders of Canada but also inspire me to continue creating meaningful and informative content.

Once again, thank you for joining me on this exploration of Canada's history, culture, and landmarks. I hope it has left you with a sense of awe and admiration for this remarkable country. Your support and feedback are truly appreciated.

Printed in Great Britain
by Amazon